ISBN: 9798300126384

The Ultimate Handbook of UI/UX Design

And How to Thrive in the age of Artificial Intelligence

TABLE OF CONTENTS

Preface: Reflections on my Career

A career in high tech is rarely a straight path—it's filled with twists, turns, and technological advancements that are often unimaginable or unpredictable. Yet, by learning from every experience, cultivating resilience, and adopting a growth mindset, it's possible to embrace each twist and turn as a new opportunity to grow and thrive.

Now that I'm entering the last phase of my career, with the busyness of raising two kids finally settling as they reach college age, I can see how the younger generation views me—often with curiosity, frequently asking for advice. It feels like both a time to reflect and a time to get excited about choosing how I want this final career phase to go.

Three Technological Revolutions

It's 2024, and we're in the midst of a technological revolution—the third one I've experienced over the three decades of my career as a digital User Experience Designer. It's hard to believe it has been 30 years. I don't feel anywhere near ready to retire. In fact, it feels like a whole new beginning, since I am learning a whole new set of skills in a new era of technological innovation. Now is, without question, the most exciting time to be a designer.

Younger readers may not realize the three "technical innovations" I'm referring to, since they've grown up with the web and smartphones. What they may not realize is that websites were not mainstream until around 1997, and capacitive touch smartphones didn't arrive until 2007.

From the Dot-Com Boom to the Age of AI

After college, my early career spanned the dot-com boom when companies were just beginning to establish a web presence, around the year 2000. Later, in my mid-career, a highlight was working as Lead Designer for mobile apps across 11 different platforms as they hit the market between 2007 and 2012. Now, I'm looking forward to what could be the ultimate career highlight as a Principal-level designer with the opportunity to grow my skills with a new range of agent capabilities powered by LLMs, NLU, and advances in storage and compute power.

As I get older, I see a new generation entering the UI/UX field, and I wonder if they can grasp the design challenges we faced 10 or 20 years ago. When I share stories about my experiences, I realize they can't fully appreciate the scale of the UX challenges I've solved as technology evolved.

Pioneering Mobile Design

Take, for instance, 2007, when I was tasked with designing my company's first-generation mobile app—before the devices had even been released to the public! There were no established design guidelines, published patterns, or best practices for designers. There was no Design Language System. We didn't have any instructions!

All we had were software emulators that we had to install on virtual machines. We would examine the native operating system and the handful of pre-installed apps, then design our app to look native to the device. It was a fun challenge because I had to recognize and mimic the patterns.

It was a whole new modality of interaction and use cases. Just as AI brings its own unique challenges today, everyone on the product team wanted to include "everything and the kitchen sink" on mobile, even when it didn't make sense. During this time, I applied User-Centered Design principles to "push back" and explain to product leaders why it was important to focus on the types of use cases people would actually *need and want* to perform on a phone as opposed to a desktop.

I also had to design for mobile conditions—on-the-go, often one-handed, perhaps holding a coffee in an elevator. There were unique limitations and new capabilities. When you think about it, these are similar to the limitations and capabilities of AI today. Like the smartphone, AI has its constraints but also introduces powerful new possibilities. Smartphones were limited by context—lighting, noise, connectivity—but had innovative features such as location services/GPS, camera, and eventually biometric authentication. Each time a new capability emerged, I had to design for it.

Not only did we have to navigate these new capabilities, but after the first iPhone was released in 2007 and the App Store opened to third-party apps in 2008, every company wanted their app in the App Store on Day One. At Citrix, I was faced with the challenge of designing our first-generation Citrix Receiver app across 11 different platforms—iOS, Android, BlackBerry, Windows Mobile, HP WebOS (Palm), and Symbian (Nokia).

iPhone was, of course, the easiest. There was only one hardware form factor, and a single operating system (OS) designed for that device. BlackBerry presented more challenges, with many variations in hardware form factors—built-in keyboards, trackballs, trackpads, slide-out keyboards, clamshell designs, etc. However, at least the hardware manufacturer was the same as the OS manufacturer, at least until Motorola released some devices with a variation of the OS.

Android was by far the most challenging OS to design for, given the variety of hardware devices with various dimensions and different custom "skinned" versions of the OS. This diversity made it hard to make our app look and feel native to each device. Imagine adding seven-inch, 10-inch, and 11-inch tablets to this mix, and you'll understand what a crazy time it was.

Even crazier was designing to allow users to interact with virtualized Windows apps and desktops on all these devices through touch gestures. I developed so many touch gesture guides to teach users how to use Windows apps on smartphones and tablets!

The years between 2007 and 2012 were by far the most rewarding and exciting of my career. It was special because I was the only designer leading mobile design during those first few years, while the technology was still new. It was less fun once the company hired more designers, and suddenly everyone was a "mobile designer."

During this time, I was able to set up a leading-edge on-site design studio equipped with high-tech equipment to bring in test participants for live usability studies. My office was also filled with devices that hadn't even been released in stores yet. My kids were young at the time, and I often brought them to work with me, where they'd play with the devices, taking photos and videos and exploring games. It was new, shiny technology that no one else had seen!

Now, returning to the purpose of writing this book—this guide is for anyone interested in a career in digital product design. Whether you're young and trying to decide if this career is right for you, or more experienced and considering a lateral move into this field, this is meant for you. I've worked with many product managers and developers who have become interested in learning about UX. In the age of YouTube and LinkedIn, there's almost nothing you can't learn. It amazes me to think we didn't have these resources 25 years ago.

A Look Back at the Start: Family Influence and Internships

Our career choices are often shaped by the experiences and opportunities we're exposed to growing up. For example, children in families with medical professionals may be guided toward the field based on that exposure. For me, I come from a family of artists and engineers. My mother's side was artistic, and my father's side was engineering-focused. It was a perfect combination for a career in user experience design—I gained an aesthetic design sense from my mother's influence and an inclination for efficiency and ease of use from my father's industrial engineering background. It wasn't until later in my career that I realized how naturally my parents' skills and influences had led me into this field.

I grew up in Connecticut, and when it came time to choose colleges and move away from home for the first time, I wanted to stay within a few hours' drive. I chose the University of Massachusetts, where I studied Industrial Engineering. My father had a thriving career at General Electric, working as an engineer and manager for 25 years. I remember stories he told me about his business trips, particularly one where he worked with Hershey's to save millions of dollars annually by simply changing the packaging on Hershey's Miniatures from a paper wrapper around foil to direct printing on the foil. Stories like this—making processes more efficient—seemed fascinating to me. I wanted to improve things, too!

I'll admit engineering was challenging, but at that time, schools were working hard to bring more women into the field (in the 90s). I had access to many resources, including joining professional organizations like the Society of Women Engineers, where I eventually became an officer. It also helped that the Dean of Engineering was a woman. At the end of my sophomore year, she helped me find a focus where I could thrive. She connected me with the BDIC program (Bachelor's Degree with Individual Concentration), and together we designed a program that incorporated Psychology and Exercise Science. My degree focus became "Human Factors and Ergonomic Engineering." Without the support of my parents and the College of Engineering, I would never have found such a fitting path. Once I found my focus, it was easy to get straight A's because I was genuinely interested in the material.

I graduated from UMass in 1993 and then attended graduate school at Penn State, where I earned my Master's in Industrial Engineering with a focus in Human Factors. After my first year—and an especially grueling winter—I noticed a bright colored flier on the graduate office bulletin board. All I saw was "FLORIDA" in big letters. The flier was for a one-year graduate student position at IBM in Boca Raton, Florida. The idea of escaping to Florida was extremely appealing, so I applied for the position.

Then, one day, I received an unexpected call. I remember I was sweeping the floor in a house I shared with two other graduate students when I heard, "This is Alan Happ from IBM." Little did I know that a single call would set the trajectory of my career.

That summer, I packed everything I owned into my little white TR7 convertible, and headed to Florida. I still remember the majestic Royal Palms lining the exit ramp off the highway as I entered Boca. For a New England girl, it seemed like a tropical paradise. I was young and inexperienced, but taking this opportunity was the pivotal step that launched my career. For high school or college students, my advice would be to take as many internship opportunities as possible. The experiences I had at a young age fueled my passion in the field.

More about internships...

Let me take a moment to describe my internship experiences and what I learned.

During college summers, I was fortunate to secure internships at Pitney Bowes, which had a dedicated Human Factors team. This gave me real-world experience working in a professional environment, and I was able to conduct usability testing on cutting-edge technology for the 90s—touch screen and speech recognition products. Since Pitney Bowes developed industrial mail processing systems, my role involved testing touchscreen mail processing software and evaluating speech recognition technology in different ambient noise conditions to mimic a mail-processing warehouse.

Fast forward to my IBM experience, which became a significant stepping stone in my career in South Florida. IBM had a thriving graduate student program. IBM covered our relocation expenses and matched us with apartments in the area. As a human factors intern, I gained experience working with actor-agent technologies—small animated assistants that helped with command and control tasks on Windows computers. I also worked with speech recognition technologies for Windows desktops, using what we called "command and control," which replaced the mouse with speech commands, as well as voice dictation.

Our studies involved "grammar capture" in a high-tech usability lab with real participants. We conducted "Wizard of Oz" studies, where participants sat on one side of a one-way mirror, completing tasks using voice commands, while we were really performing the actions on the other side of the glass. I have some funny stories from those times, like when I accidentally performed the actions before the participant spoke, leading them to think it was telepathy, unaware we were observing from the other side. Of course, we debriefed participants afterward, and they were always surprised!

IBM: The Opportunity That Shaped My Career

As an intern, I was responsible for all aspects of running usability studies, from planning, recruiting participants, and facilitating the study to analyzing and presenting findings. Because we were testing the products daily, we became experts at certain things, like tuning the microphone for optimal performance. I even designed a microphone wizard that was included with the product to ensure users' success.

Luckily, I had a strong work ethic back then and often arrived at the office early and stayed late. One day, this work ethic paid off—I was staying late, and everyone else had left. Around 6 p.m., one of the executives rushed down the hallway with a panicked expression. He asked, "Do you know how to get the microphone working?" Apparently, he was on a call with a prominent technology reporter from *InfoWorld*, and the reporter was having trouble with the software. Since I ran extensive usability studies in the lab, I knew the software inside and out, so I guided the reporter on how to fix the microphone over the phone. Until that moment, I had been invisible to this executive. But just by being in the right place at the right time, he now knew my name. I had saved the day.

These are the unexpected moments that unlock opportunities. Now, let me tell you how that moment opened up my next opportunity.

Fast forward about a year. I had finished my classes at Penn State and moved back to Florida to take on a full-time position at IBM. This was initially just a contract job, paid hourly without the benefits of a salaried employee—no medical insurance, paid time off, or benefits like 401k matching. I saw it as a valuable way to get my foot in the door at IBM, setting myself up for a full-time salaried position. I maintained a great working relationship with the executive, and I would occasionally stop by to ask if there was any new information about when a full-time position might be available.

Then one day, I received a call for a "top secret" meeting. The mysterious caller asked me to sign an NDA and meet in a downstairs conference room. During the meeting, I learned that this executive wanted to offer me a full-time position as Lead Designer for a brand-new startup company. Not only that, but IBM had recently moved to West Palm Beach, so I had been commuting an hour each day from Boca Raton. This new opportunity was right in my hometown, with offices on Ocean Blvd overlooking the ocean! Knowing I was waiting for a full-time role with benefits, they extended an offer to join the startup. This marked the beginning of my four-year adventure in the dot-com startup era.

The Dot-Com Startup Era: Building Skills and Learning on the Job

During the dot-com boom, many executives took early retirement and left large companies to form small dot-com startups. From 1997 to 2001, I worked for two startups: one was a voice-driven IVR company, and the other a web-based e-commerce micropayment system. One of these companies went public; the other ran out of money just before it could.

I firmly believe that "no experience is a bad experience." We learn and grow from every experience, and I can look back now and see how much I grew during that time. In the first startup, I wore many hats, gaining new skills along the way. Not only did I design interaction conversation flows for telephony products (like call centers and personal assistants), but I also set up an on-site recording studio, scripted voice prompts, hired voice talent, coached and recorded the actors in the studio, and digitally edited all the prompts to prepare them for production. Looking back, I am amazed at what I accomplished. These are things you don't learn in college—you only gain them through on-the-job training.

After three years, the company went public, and I was able to cash in my 1,500 shares of stock, which allowed me to pay off my car. Unfortunately, the company later went through a reverse merger and ultimately closed its doors.

For my next two jobs, I didn't even have to search or apply. There was a close-knit network of IBMers in the Boca Raton area back then, so as soon as one opportunity ended, I was contacted about the next one. I moved to a new startup and negotiated a great deal for shares of stock in case the company went public. About a month before the anticipated IPO, the company ran out of money and could not pay its employees. I suspect there was some corruption among the partners due to significant drama, but I was too young and naive to fully understand it at the time. Eventually, I submitted a resignation letter and walked out, and within two weeks, the rest of the product development team followed suit. They later asked me to rescind my resignation to receive back pay. My dad always said, "If it sounds too good to be true, then it probably is." I still have the original stock certificate for 25,000 shares tucked away in my file cabinet, a reminder of my dream of what could have been a quarter of a million dollars.

Not long after this happened in 2001, another former IBM colleague reached out with an opportunity in Boca. The role was Senior Usability Engineer at NTT/Verio. Ironically, the office was back at IBM's former campus, where I had worked a few years earlier. Interviewing was relatively easy because they already knew they wanted me before I met the manager. In this role, I conducted heuristic usability reviews and studies on web hosting consoles, both consumer-facing (B2C) and for our resellers (B2B). I created use case specifications, identified users' goals and tasks, developed user flows and wireframes, and conducted usability testing. I reported results to developers, advising them on how to make the products more intuitive.

Three years later, however, the company went through a massive layoff and eliminated the UX team.

A New Start at Citrix and Navigating Enterprise UX

In 2004, I went through my first "cold" interview with Citrix in Fort Lauderdale. I had a baby boy at home, and since I was the primary breadwinner, I needed to return to work. This was the first time I ever had to prepare for an interview. Luckily, Citrix was forming a new team, so I was able to get in on the ground floor of the newly formed Human Factors and Design team (as it was called then). I spent 10 years as a designer at Citrix, and I consider this my first real career growth working for an enterprise SaaS B2B company. During that time, our team grew from six to 20 people in the first five years, establishing specialized roles and career tracks. I'll discuss levels and career paths later in this book.

Around 2012, the company made a significant investment in UX by hiring a C-suite executive as VP of Design. Up until that point, UX reported up through Product Management, so we had to do a lot of work to champion the value of User-Centered Design. Our new VP transformed the company from product-focused to design-focused and rolled out a "Design Matters to Me" campaign, which refocused everyone's role on what matters to our customers. Suddenly the team was elevated and we had a seat at the table in driving the product roadmap. I remember having cabinets full of Citrix Design Team swag with our "Design Matters to Me" tagline on it. This period, between 2007 and 2012, was a golden age for design, during the dawn of mobile smartphones and tablets.

Over the ten years I spent at Citrix, our User-Centered Design practice grew and matured. We evolved into a well-functioning, multidisciplinary team with specialized roles and titles. Each career path had defined levels, which I'll talk about later in the book. My title was Lead Product Designer, meaning I was in charge of managing all the UX activities that would shape the user experience for my product lines.

As Lead Product Designer, I planned and managed all the UX activities from concept to delivery. I was responsible for the interaction design, producing wireframes, and collaborating with a visual designer to create the branded look—graphical treatments and assets. I was the Lead Designer for two of Citrix's flagship products: Citrix Receiver and Citrix XenMobile, which managed the delivery and security of corporate apps on any device.

This period saw a major shift in enterprise software with the advent of BYOD—"Bring Your Own Device." Companies were saving money by allowing employees to access corporate desktops and applications from their own personal devices, which introduced a whole new set of challenges for securing those resources and keeping work and personal data separate. I designed the IT security configurations surrounding network, user, and device security, as well as interactions on devices to control access to corporate applications. This included geofencing and mobile device management (MDM) capabilities that were emerging at the time.

I designed the look and feel of the product on nearly every platform imaginable, including desktop OSs (Windows, Apple, Chromebook, Linux) and mobile OSs (iOS, Android, Windows Mobile, BlackBerry, webOS, Symbian). Citrix had a "day one" strategy, aiming to have a Citrix app in every app store on the very day it opened to the public. This created a unique challenge for designers—we had to design an app that was recognizable as Citrix but tailored to look and feel native to each OS, and we had to design it before the devices were even available to the public. It was a hectic time, but thankfully the mobile device market eventually settled down to Mac and Windows for desktop, and iOS and Android for mobile.

This was an exciting period, as I learned a wide range of technologies and tackled interesting challenges in this role. I also had my second child in 2006 and was a working mom, raising two kids while at Citrix. In the last four years under our new VP of Design, we were able to build on-site design studios and equip them with any technology we needed. We had great Design Summit events, and I often flew to Santa Clara for Design Sprint Workshops with various Product Leaders.

Toastmasters: A Pivotal Decision to Get Out of my Comfort Zone

Public speaking was one of my biggest roadblocks to career advancement throughout college and my early career. While at Citrix, I grew tired of the anxiety I felt whenever I had to speak at meetings or events, so I decided to confront my fear by joining Citrix Toastmasters, a public speaking club. I committed to completing the entire program, including both the Competent Communicator and Leadership tracks. Overcoming my fear of public speaking was one of the hardest things I've ever done, but also the most rewarding. Forcing myself to step out of my comfort zone allowed me to build confidence and stop hiding from my fear.

The club met once a week after work, and people participated as much or as little as they felt comfortable. The first part of the meeting was called Table Topics, where random topics were drawn from a box, and each person would speak for two minutes on the chosen topic, completely unscripted. In the second part of the meeting, participants delivered speeches that were part of Toastmasters' self-paced curriculum, with each speech focusing on a different skill—like body language, comedy, persuasion, and audience connection. Surprisingly, the hardest speech was the first one entitled, "Tell me About Yourself". Every speech was timed according to the program's rules, so not only did you have to design the speech, but you also had to practice your delivery and present at the front of the room.

Through Toastmasters, I learned to redirect my anxiety into positive energy. Before Toastmasters, I missed out on opportunities because of fear, but confronting that fear was the best gift I could give myself.

Throughout my career, there have been pivotal decisions like this that propelled me forward in personal and professional growth. I committed to completing the program, no matter how I felt. I think I was also tired of missing out on opportunities that were going to less competent people who were simply more confident.

Then came the layoffs in 2015, which shocked everyone. Thankfully, with 10 years of seniority, I received a decent severance package. However, I was still the breadwinner, supporting a family of four with a mortgage, and my kids were deeply embedded in the local school system, so relocating wasn't an option. It was clear that this layoff was a cost-cutting measure, eliminating higher-seniority employees and replacing them with entry-level positions. The company took a big hit, losing a lot of institutional knowledge.

Thank you for a great 10 years, Citrix. Next.

Post-Layoff Challenges, Resilience & Growth

Looking back, I honestly don't know how I managed to keep it together. It was incredibly challenging trying to do a job search and present my best self while also managing young kids. Another reason it was difficult was that I hadn't kept my resume or portfolio up-to-date, and I had little experience with interviewing or marketing myself. I particularly dreaded panel interviews, but thankfully I had invested in myself by completing the Toastmasters program while at Citrix.

The phase of my career between Citrix and Ultimate Software was by far the most challenging. Reflecting on it, I feel proud of the decisions I made and the strong work ethic that got me through this time and ultimately helped me land my dream job.

Having been in a Lead Product Designer position, responsible for managing all UX activities for two major product lines at Citrix, I felt confident in my hands-on and leadership skills in User-Centered Design. My first mistake was rushing to apply for jobs without first putting together a polished portfolio website or spending time to refine my resume. I quickly realized that people expected a professional portfolio website, which would become their first impression, beyond just my skills designing enterprise software. I learned this lesson the hard way, and after a few bruised ego moments, I decided to invest time into creating a stylish website to showcase my work samples. Although it was time-consuming and costly, requiring web hosting and a Squarespace template, it was ultimately worth it. I realized that I would be judged on the experience of the portfolio website more than my actual skills in the UX process.

In the months after the Citrix layoff, I gained new insights. I had never had to "sell" myself to people who didn't already know me. Initially, I approached interviews with confidence, only to be humbled by lukewarm responses. This slice of "humble pie" motivated me to work harder on organizing my work into a visually appealing website to prove my value. I'm not the most charismatic person—I'm neither a salesperson nor a marketer—so I wasn't great at advertising myself. I struggled to market myself effectively to new organizations that didn't already know my skills from my work.

As my severance funds began to dwindle, I worked fervently on my portfolio and resume. There weren't many tech companies in South Florida at the time, and most opportunities required relocation, which wasn't feasible with my kids. Then, one of those pivotal, unexpected moments arrived.

I was sitting in the bleachers at my son's softball game (he was about 10 at the time), working on my laptop, when another parent asked what I was doing. This sparked a conversation about my job search, and he mentioned meeting someone in an airport lounge who was starting a new company in Fort Lauderdale and was struggling to find good technical people. He gave me the contact information, and I did something completely out of my comfort zone—I cold-called the CEO. The company was developing IoT (Internet of Things) technology solutions. In my conversation with the CEO, I learned they had just hired a handful of developers and planned to create leading-edge track and trace solutions for industries like healthcare, retail, grocery, and manufacturing.

This led to an on-site meeting where, armed with a whiteboard marker, I pitched why the company needed a UX Designer to design solutions for their clients. I explained that their developers alone couldn't succeed without a sound User-Centered Design process, and that I could help them understand client needs and design solutions to meet those needs. I managed to convince them to create this position, and they hired me as a contractor for a few months until the company's grand opening.

I was optimistic that after the contract period, I'd receive a full-time offer comparable to my Citrix salary. However, as the conversion date neared, the CTO kept stalling and suggested discussing my conversion to full-time over dinner, which felt uncomfortable. I sensed ulterior motives and tried to avoid an awkward situation. Finally, at the last possible moment before my COBRA medical benefits expired, the CTO offered me a salary that was much lower than what I had earned at Citrix. Although this was unethical on his part, I was forced into a corner, needing a job to support my family and medical benefits, so I accepted the offer.

People closest to me criticized my decision, but I had a plan. The position allowed me to work on cutting-edge technology products and create impressive demos for clients, making for a "sexy" portfolio. I made the decision to embrace the opportunity, and turned every project into a portfolio piece, meticulously documenting each phase from concept to delivery. I would arrive early, roll the whiteboard over to my desk, and conduct pseudo workshopping. If I didn't have time to complete every UX phase, I filled in the blanks myself. Not only did I go above and beyond on every project, which helped the company demo products live to investors in a state-of-the-art technology showroom, but I also built a strong portfolio.

I called 2016 my "Year of the Job Search." My mission was to enhance my portfolio and secure as many interview opportunities as possible, aiming to return to a reputable company. Every interview was a chance to refine my "advertisement", step out of my comfort zone, observe, adjust, and improve. Finally, my mission paid off. By the end of 2016, I landed a job with the "other big technology company" in South Florida—Ultimate Software. I had interviewed with them three times in 2016, but the first two positions closed due to restructuring. Then, in

November, the hiring manager who knew me from previous interviews reached out, offering a position at a $20K pay raise.

Transitioning to Ultimate Software and Growing as an Enterprise UX Leader

Finally! All my hard work paid off. Not only did I gain a fantastic professional growth opportunity as the sole UX Designer for a high-tech startup, but I also had the rewarding experience of landing my dream job at my dream company through patience, perseverance, and hard work. I had grown immensely from the experience of being laid off and the personal and professional challenges it brought.

As I write this, I am approaching my eight year work anniversary with my current company.. When I chose this career, I didn't anticipate changing companies so frequently, but I learned early on that, in high tech, change is constant. Companies evolve with technological advancements, reorganizing and adapting as the business landscape shifts. I also observed that people who move from company to company advance more quickly in their careers. For me, I've chosen to stay in the same location to provide stability for my kids, which has meant a slower career progression compared to those who relocate to tech hubs.

I'm happy to be with my current company for eight years, and although I've stayed in one place, I've experienced tremendous reorganization and change. This isn't only due to internal shifts; external factors, such as the global pandemic, have drastically changed the way we work. I was hired at Ultimate Software in 2016 as Lead Product Designer for the company's HR product. At that time, the Enterprise UX team was centralized, meaning we were a "shared resource" across product lines, so while Lead Designers were supporting product lines, the reporting structure was outside the product line.

About eight months after I started, the product development team reorganized, which created smaller dedicated UX teams into each product line. Lead Product Designers were encouraged to apply to the newly formed UX Manager roles. After applying for this role for teams based locally, they asked if I would manage the UX team for a product line based in Toronto, Canada. Apparently, as I found out later, the Director of that product line was considered difficult to work with. They thought my personality would be a good fit for navigating this challenge since I was coming in without knowledge of past conflicts and could offer a fresh start.

It turned out to be a successful match. Over the next two years, I established User-Centered Design processes and best practices for the team, and was able to grow the team to five designers and a researcher. Since none of my team was based in Florida, I mostly worked remotely, although I still visited the local office on Thursdays to reconnect with designers over lunch.

This was probably the best period of my career. I managed an effective design team working on our next-generation Workforce Management product while also supporting our existing legacy products. We conducted extensive user research, ran design sprint workshops, and even flew the entire Product Management team to Florida for a three-day journey mapping and ideation workshop. My Director at the time was a great mentor and role model, involving the entire team in developing initiatives to drive business success. He kept us informed on

Critical Success Factors for the business and KPI metrics that demonstrated how our work contributed to the company's vision. I appreciated this exposure to the business side of things, something I hadn't experienced before.

Working for such a strong leader inspired me to start my MBA journey. I wanted to develop a stronger business acumen as I moved up the corporate ladder, enabling me to better measure the impact of our UX work on business outcomes. I felt that having a business background would help me more effectively represent the ROI of design in an enterprise setting.

Embracing Change: The UKG Merger and Shift to a Remote Workforce

2020 was a unique year. Not only did the pandemic hit, but the company was also acquired by a private equity firm and merged with another company, Kronos, forming a new entity—UKG (Ultimate Kronos Group). The merger closed on April 1, 2020, right after both companies went 100% remote. Amidst all this, I had begun my MBA classes and was fully committed to the program. My kids were in middle and high school, which brought its own set of challenges with school closures.

In 2021, the company announced it was "sunsetting" the product line I was working on because it would be replaced by the flagship product of the merged company. This decision made sense, as the other company had a very mature enterprise product. Consequently, they dissolved the UX Team I managed, and I returned to an individual contributor (IC) role, with my title changing to Principal UX/Product Designer. Shortly afterward, I transitioned to the new product line alongside a handful of designers from the other company.

Then, in March 2022, UKG announced a return-to-office policy requiring employees to come back three days a week. Returning to the office wasn't the same as it had been pre-pandemic. There were no more assigned seats, so we had to set up our workspace each time we came in. Pre-pandemic, coming to the office felt like a luxury—you could personalize your space and keep items like a box of tissues, a picture frame, or a plant on your desk.

Since then, we've experienced multiple company reorganizations, including two rounds of layoffs. Thankfully, I've weathered these changes and am now positioned to be part of the new AI movement. One advantage of being on the UX team of a leading-edge cloud enterprise software company is the abundance of opportunities to grow and learn. We have a wealth of resources for learning new technologies, including AI agents and large language models (LLMs). Recently, I participated in a company hackathon, where I used the latest AI technology to develop a prototype that automates the customer feedback loop. When a customer has a question or issue, the AI assistant engages in an empathetic conversation, offers an immediate solution, and simultaneously sends the feedback to our Product Leadership team to help improve the product. The AI agent continually learns and evolves. My prototype won First Place!

Embracing a Growth Mindset: My MBA Journey and New Opportunities in AI

Over the past year, I've truly embraced a growth mindset, setting a mission to learn the latest AI technologies. This is an exciting time to be a designer, as we can use our skills to identify user needs and business problems, applying AI technologies to unlock a whole new range of solutions. I've not only come to love AI tools that augment my work and make my personal life easier, but I've also discovered a passion for creating AI agents that can automate repetitive, monotonous, or inefficient tasks.

As I enter this later stage of my career, I am thrilled to bring all my skills together and look forward to new opportunities in this technological revolution. I'll be completing my MBA in 2025, and I'm excited about the career advancement opportunities that will open up. I'm also diving deeply into AI agent technologies and look forward to exploring new business opportunities they will offer.

01 The Evolution of UI/UX Design

The world of UI/UX design has come a long way—from its early days as a niche interest in the tech world to today, where it's a defining element of almost every digital product we use. What's interesting about UI/UX design isn't just the progress in how we design experiences but also how we talk about it. The evolution of terminology—from "Human Factors Engineer" to "UI/UX Designer" and beyond—reflects both the changing skills in the field and the broader recognition of the importance of design for user-centered products. Let's dive into this journey of shifting titles, expanding roles, and growing recognition for what UI/UX designers do.

The Early Days: From Ergonomics to HCI

The earliest roots of UI/UX design reach back to the fields of industrial design and ergonomics in the early 20th century. At that time, designers and engineers sought to improve how people interacted with everything from cars to household tools. They focused on "human factors," aiming to make products that fit the human body and mind. Job titles like "Human Factors Engineer" or "Ergonomics Specialist" emerged, particularly in fields like aviation and manufacturing, where there was a clear need to make complex equipment safer and more intuitive to use.

By the 1960s and 1970s, as computers began to enter workplaces, the field of Human-Computer Interaction (HCI) came into existence, bringing with it roles like "Human-Computer Interaction Specialist" and "Human Factors Engineer." These roles were primarily focused on making computers more accessible and effective for their human users, an idea that sounds obvious now but was groundbreaking at the time. This work laid the groundwork for what would later evolve into both UI and UX design, even though the technology at the time was far from what we use today.

Interface Design and the Rise of Graphic Designers: 1980s–1990s

The tech boom of the 1980s and the release of personal computers brought a new focus on interface design. With computers like Apple's Macintosh debuting the graphical user interface (GUI), the need for screens that were visually appealing and easy to navigate became essential. "Interface Designer" and "Graphic Designer" roles became prominent in companies like Apple, Microsoft, and IBM, focusing on making computer screens that were not only functional but also visually clear.

In the 1990s, as the web exploded, the role of the "Web Designer" gained popularity. Web designers combined elements of graphic design with the technical knowledge required to create functional websites, although at that time, the focus was largely on layout and aesthetics rather than user-centered interaction. Usability became a buzzword, thanks to pioneers like Jakob Nielsen, who introduced usability principles that encouraged designers to think more about how people used products, not just how they looked [Nielsen, 1993].

Enter User Experience: 2000s and the UX Boom

In the early 2000s, the term "User Experience" (or UX) began to surface, thanks in large part to cognitive scientist Donald Norman, who worked at Apple and advocated for a holistic view of design that went beyond aesthetics to include every touchpoint in a user's interaction with a product [Norman, 2004]. Titles like "User Experience Designer" or simply "UX Designer" emerged, focusing not just on how something looked or functioned, but on the entire experience it provided to users, including emotional responses and ease of use.

As digital products became more sophisticated, companies recognized that the visual layer (UI) and the experience layer (UX) were interconnected but required different skill sets. This realization led to more specific job titles: "User Interface Designer" focused on the visual side of things—colors, typography, button styles—while "User Experience Designer" encompassed user research, information architecture, and prototyping. These roles began to reflect the full journey users would take when interacting with a product, encouraging a more comprehensive approach to design.

The Rise of UI/UX and Product Design: 2010s and Beyond

By the 2010s, it was common for companies to want designers who could do both UI and UX work, leading to the now-popular title "UI/UX Designer." This hybrid role expects a designer to balance both the visual design and the experience aspects of a product. Many companies, especially startups, favor this combined title as it implies versatility. However, in larger organizations, UI and UX roles often remain separate to allow deeper specialization.

At the same time, more nuanced roles emerged as design took on even broader responsibilities within product development. "Product Designer" became a popular title, reflecting a designer who considers the entire product lifecycle from a strategic, user-centered perspective. Product Designers are expected to understand the business goals behind a product, work cross-functionally with development and marketing teams, and make design decisions that align with larger company objectives. Meanwhile, the title "Visual Designer" emerged as an evolution of the graphic designer, with a stronger focus on digital interfaces and branding.

Current Landscape: A Spectrum of Specialized Roles

Today, UI/UX design is often used as an umbrella term, but the field includes a wide range of specialized roles. Job titles like "Interaction Designer," "UX Researcher," "Content Strategist," and "Service

Designer" are common, each reflecting a particular focus within the broader field of user-centered design. Interaction Designers concentrate on the ways users interact with elements on a screen, while UX Researchers conduct in-depth studies to understand user behaviors and needs. Content Strategists ensure that the language and flow of information match user needs, while Service Designers map out complex user journeys across different touchpoints, both digital and physical.

The increasing complexity of digital products has driven demand for these more specialized roles, as they allow for deeper focus on individual aspects of the user experience. However, titles like "UI/UX Designer" and "Product Designer" remain popular, especially in smaller companies, where designers are often expected to wear multiple hats and bring both broad and flexible skill sets to the table.

Looking Ahead: New Frontiers in Design Titles

As emerging technologies like AI, augmented reality, and voice interfaces gain popularity, we're likely to see the rise of new design roles, perhaps focused on areas like "Voice UI Designer" or "AI Interaction Designer." These roles will need to tackle unique challenges around user trust, privacy, and non-visual interaction. In addition, the emphasis on ethical design is leading to new discussions around roles like "Ethical Experience Designer," which may soon become common titles as companies work to balance innovation with social responsibility.

In summary, the evolution of job titles in UI/UX design reflects both the field's growth and the increasing recognition of design as a vital part of product development. What started as a focus on visual layout and simple interactions has become a diverse field, covering every touchpoint of the user experience. For aspiring UI/UX designers, understanding this journey and the variety of roles available today can help you navigate the career path that best aligns with your skills and interests.

The progression of UI/UX job titles is more than just a list of names—it tells a story about how the field has transformed to better serve the people using the products we design. As the roles evolve, so too does the potential to create even richer, more intuitive user experiences.

02 User-Centered Design (UCD) Methodology

User-Centered Design (UCD) is more than just a set of steps—it's a mindset. It's about putting the user at the heart of every design decision and crafting products that genuinely meet people's needs, wants, and expectations. UCD is one of the most respected and widely practiced methodologies in the world of design, guiding how designers think, research, create, and iterate. For anyone considering a career in UI/UX design, understanding UCD is essential, as it provides the framework for building products that are not only functional but also enjoyable and accessible.

This chapter explores the principles, processes, and practices of User-Centered Design, breaking down how this approach shapes the work of designers and leads to user experiences that resonate.

The Foundations of User-Centered Design

User-Centered Design emerged from the early work in human factors and ergonomics, evolving through disciplines like Human-Computer Interaction (HCI) and cognitive psychology. Donald Norman, one of the leading figures in the field, helped popularize UCD by emphasizing the importance of understanding users' goals, motivations, and pain points to create products that work *for* people, not just *with* people [Norman, 1988].

At its core, UCD is about empathy. It's an approach that prioritizes understanding the user's context, limitations, and needs, encouraging designers to develop solutions that align with real-world usage. UCD is also iterative, meaning it views design as a constantly evolving process where feedback and insights guide continuous improvements. By maintaining a focus on the end user, UCD ensures that every decision, from the color of a button to the layout of a navigation menu, has purpose and meaning.

Key Principles of User-Centered Design

Several foundational principles guide the UCD approach, providing designers with a set of "north stars" as they create user-focused experiences.

1. **Early and Continuous Focus on Users**
   UCD emphasizes involving users from the very beginning of the design process and continuously throughout development. The idea is to bring users' voices into the design as early as

possible and to ensure that their feedback influences each iteration. This often involves regular user testing, interviews, surveys, and observations, ensuring that design decisions are based on real user input rather than assumptions or biases.

2. **Understanding the Full Context of Use**
   UCD looks beyond the screen or device to consider the broader context in which the product will be used. This includes understanding the users' physical, social, and technological environments, which helps create a more relevant and tailored experience. For example, if designing a mobile app for drivers, UCD would encourage designers to account for environmental distractions and limited physical interaction with the device.

3. **Iteration and Feedback Loops**
   One of the hallmarks of UCD is that it embraces an iterative process, incorporating regular user feedback to refine and improve designs over time. Each iteration is seen as an opportunity to validate assumptions, test ideas, and resolve any issues that may arise in usability or functionality. This cycle continues until the product reaches a point where it meets the intended user experience goals.

4. **Designing for Usability and Accessibility**
   UCD ensures that products are usable, accessible, and functional for a broad spectrum of users, including those with disabilities or limitations. It encourages designers to think about inclusivity from the outset, ensuring that no user is left behind and that the product can be accessed and enjoyed by as many people as possible.

The User-Centered Design Process

The UCD process is often broken down into a series of stages, which, while flexible, offer a clear roadmap for designing with users at the center. Though these stages may vary slightly depending on the methodology or framework used, the general steps include research, design, testing, and iteration.

1. **Research and Discovery**
   UCD begins with in-depth research to understand users' needs, behaviors, and pain points. This phase often involves techniques like user interviews, focus groups, surveys, and contextual observations. Designers aim to gain as much insight as possible into users' challenges, motivations, and goals, as well as the competitive landscape, to identify opportunities for differentiation.

   A common output of this stage is the creation of user personas and user journey maps. Personas are fictional characters based on real user data that represent key user types, while journey maps illustrate how users interact with a product over time, identifying critical touchpoints and moments of friction.

2. **Ideation and Concept Development**
   Once designers understand users, they move into ideation, brainstorming potential solutions and concepts that address the identified needs. This phase is about exploring possibilities, encouraging creative thinking, and focusing on quantity over quality to generate a range of ideas. Collaborative workshops like sketching sessions or design sprints can be helpful here, as

they allow cross-functional teams to work together to generate ideas that might not emerge in isolation.

3. **Prototyping and Design**

   With a clear direction established, designers move into creating low-fidelity prototypes, wireframes, or sketches to begin visualizing the ideas in a tangible format. Early prototypes allow designers to test the structure and flow without investing too much time in details, helping them focus on usability and functionality. As the design matures, higher-fidelity mockups and prototypes are created, incorporating branding, color schemes, and interaction elements.

4. **User Testing and Evaluation**

   User testing is a critical stage in UCD, as it provides a reality check for assumptions made during the design process. By observing real users interacting with the product, designers gain insights into what works, what doesn't, and where users encounter challenges. Testing methods may include usability tests, A/B testing, and feedback sessions, all of which help validate design choices and highlight areas that need refinement. During testing, designers gather both qualitative and quantitative data, which inform adjustments and improvements to the design. This phase may reveal unexpected behaviors or pain points, and it encourages an open-minded approach to solving design problems.

5. **Iteration and Refinement**

   Based on user feedback, the design is refined, addressing any pain points or usability issues that emerged during testing. This iterative cycle—design, test, refine—continues until the product meets the defined usability goals and provides a satisfying user experience. The iterative nature of UCD ensures that designers remain adaptable, willing to change directions based on real-world insights rather than pushing forward with a preconceived solution.

UCD in Practice: Tools and Techniques

User-Centered Design incorporates various tools and techniques to support each stage of the process. Some commonly used methods include:

- **Personas and Empathy Maps:** These tools help designers capture user characteristics, goals, and needs, allowing them to keep user priorities front and center throughout the design.
- **Wireframes and Prototypes:** These visual representations range from simple sketches to clickable prototypes, enabling designers to test and refine ideas at different stages.
- **Usability Testing:** Through observing real users, designers gather critical insights that help validate design choices and highlight areas that need improvement.
- **Feedback Surveys and Interviews:** Direct user feedback provides designers with qualitative insights into the user experience, helping inform decisions on the product's evolution.
- **Journey Mapping:** Mapping out user interactions over time reveals opportunities to improve user flows and address potential pain points in the experience.

Why User-Centered Design Matters

User-Centered Design is so much more than a checklist—it's a philosophy that prioritizes understanding, empathy, and adaptation. In today's competitive digital landscape, UCD is essential for creating products that stand out by genuinely serving their users. By taking the time to understand the people they're designing for, UI/UX professionals create experiences that not only meet functional needs but also bring value and satisfaction to users' lives.

For aspiring UI/UX designers, adopting a UCD mindset means staying committed to the user's perspective, embracing iteration, and always being open to feedback. As the field continues to evolve, User-Centered Design will remain a foundational approach, ensuring that design is never about simply making things look good—it's about making things work for people.

By placing the user at the center, UCD brings purpose to every design choice. For those entering the field, mastering this approach will provide a strong foundation for creating meaningful, user-first experiences in an ever-evolving digital world.

03 Research and Discovery

Research and discovery are the essential starting points in the User-Centered Design (UCD) process. Before we can design meaningful and effective user experiences, we need to understand the people we're designing for—how they think, what they need, what motivates them, and where they encounter frustrations. This phase sets the foundation for every design decision that follows, providing insights that drive user-centered solutions.

In this chapter, we'll explore the tools, techniques, and methodologies that guide designers through the research and discovery phase, highlighting how each contributes to a deeper understanding of users and a more focused design process.

The Purpose of Research and Discovery

The goal of research and discovery is to gather as much relevant information about users and their environments as possible, ideally uncovering insights that will lead to a more intuitive, effective design. Research is critical for surfacing user needs, identifying pain points, and defining requirements for the product. Without it, designers risk building products based on assumptions or personal preferences rather than actual user needs.

The research and discovery process also enables designers to:

- **Define the target audience** with precision, understanding demographic details, motivations, and behaviors.
- **Identify and prioritize user needs**, ensuring that the design addresses real-world challenges.
- **Map the user journey**, highlighting key touchpoints, emotions, and possible friction points.
- **Validate assumptions** and replace biases with data-driven insights.

Research Methods in User-Centered Design

The research phase includes a mix of qualitative and quantitative methods to capture a well-rounded view of user experiences. Each method offers different insights, and using a combination provides a fuller picture of user needs.

1. User Interviews

Purpose: Direct conversations with users reveal rich, qualitative insights into their motivations, goals, and frustrations. User interviews are especially useful for gathering in-depth information about users' experiences, as they allow designers to explore the "why" behind certain behaviors and preferences.

Process: Interviews are typically conducted one-on-one, often using open-ended questions to encourage users to share freely. These conversations may cover topics like users' daily routines, their use of similar products, and specific challenges they face.

Advantages:

- Provides detailed, personal insights into user needs and emotions.
- Allows follow-up questions to clarify or explore specific points.

Challenges:

- Time-consuming and may require skilled interviewers to avoid leading questions.
- Qualitative data may be harder to generalize.

2. Surveys and Questionnaires

Purpose: Surveys are effective for gathering quantitative data from a large group of users, helping to identify trends and preferences within a target audience. They're often used to validate findings from interviews, as they allow for broader sampling.

Process: Surveys are typically designed with both closed-ended questions (for easy quantification) and open-ended questions (to allow for richer responses). Online survey tools like Google Forms or SurveyMonkey are commonly used.

Advantages:

- Cost-effective for reaching a large audience.
- Provides statistically relevant data when used with a large sample.

Challenges:

- Responses may lack depth.
- Survey design can introduce bias, especially with leading or confusing questions.

3. Focus Groups

Purpose: Focus groups bring together a small group of users to discuss a product or concept in a guided discussion, providing a forum for users to share their perspectives and even build on each other's ideas. This method can be helpful for generating insights into group dynamics and shared experiences.

Process: A facilitator leads the discussion, encouraging participants to share opinions on specific aspects of the product or design concept. It's common to use focus groups in the early stages to test reactions to new ideas or features.

Advantages:

- Allows for real-time feedback and group discussion.
- Enables designers to observe group dynamics and interaction.

Challenges:

- Risk of groupthink, where participants conform to dominant opinions.
- Responses may not reflect individual experiences accurately.

4. Contextual Inquiry

Purpose: Contextual inquiry involves observing users in their natural environment, providing an authentic view of how they interact with a product in real-world settings. This method is particularly useful for understanding workflow, context, and behaviors that users might overlook when simply describing their experiences.

Process: Designers or researchers observe users as they interact with the product or service, asking clarifying questions to understand their actions and decisions. Often, contextual inquiry uses a "master-apprentice" model, where the user "teaches" the researcher about their routine or processes.

Advantages:

- Reveals insights about real-world use cases and environments.
- Highlights unspoken or subconscious behaviors.

Challenges:

- Requires careful observation and can be time-consuming.
- May require permission or coordination for workplace settings.

5. Diary Studies

Purpose: Diary studies are a long-term approach where users document their experiences, thoughts, and interactions with a product over days or weeks. This method is valuable for understanding how user interactions and perceptions evolve over time.

Process: Participants record their thoughts in a diary (physical or digital) each time they interact with the product, often including details about their mood, environment, and tasks. Designers review the entries to understand the product's role in the users' daily lives.

Advantages:

- Provides insights into long-term engagement and behavioral patterns.
- Allows users to self-reflect and capture detailed context.

Challenges:

- High participant effort required, leading to possible drop-off.
- Self-reporting can introduce bias.

6. Competitive Analysis

Purpose: This technique involves analyzing competitors' products to identify strengths, weaknesses, and potential gaps in the market. Competitive analysis helps designers understand industry standards and discover ways to differentiate their product.

Process: Designers or researchers evaluate competitor products for usability, features, design trends, and user feedback. This process often includes creating a comparative matrix to visualize the differences and similarities.

Advantages:

- Provides insight into user expectations based on industry standards.
- Identifies opportunities for unique or improved features.

Challenges:

- Requires access to competitor products.
- Risk of overemphasizing competitor features instead of focusing on unique user needs.

Tools Used in the Research and Discovery Phase

To support these research methods, designers often rely on a variety of digital tools. Each tool is tailored to different aspects of research, from user interviews to survey analysis.

- **Survey Tools:** Google Forms, SurveyMonkey, and Typeform help designers create, distribute, and analyze surveys.
- **Interview and Focus Group Tools:** Zoom, Otter.ai, and Miro are helpful for remote interviews and focus group discussions, offering options for transcription, recording, and collaborative note-taking.
- **Usability Testing Tools:** UserTesting, Lookback, and Maze facilitate remote usability tests, allowing designers to observe users in real-time or analyze recordings.
- **Competitive Analysis Tools:** Tools like Crayon and Kompyte track competitor activity and provide insights on features, marketing, and design trends.
- **Diary Study Tools:** Tools like Dscout and ExperienceFellow support remote diary studies, offering prompts, submission tracking, and user feedback analysis.

Synthesizing Research Findings

After conducting research, designers need to synthesize their findings into actionable insights. This step often involves creating visual summaries that capture the essence of the research and translate it into tangible design requirements.

1. Personas and Empathy Maps

Personas are fictional representations of key user types, based on real user data. They provide a human-centered way of organizing research insights, capturing characteristics, goals, and needs of different user groups. Empathy maps, on the other hand, focus on users' thoughts, feelings, actions, and needs, helping designers view the product from the user's perspective.

2. User Journey Maps

User journey maps plot the steps a user takes to accomplish a task or goal, from initial awareness to the final outcome. This technique highlights the user's pain points and touchpoints, making it easier for designers to see where improvements are needed in the experience.

3. Affinity Diagrams

An affinity diagram groups related research insights, making it easier to see patterns or themes that emerge from qualitative data. This approach is particularly helpful for organizing notes from interviews or open-ended survey responses, allowing designers to identify common threads.

Why Research and Discovery Matter in UCD

Research and discovery serve as the foundation of the User-Centered Design process, equipping designers with a deep understanding of who they're designing for and why. By committing to thorough research, designers not only gain a clearer picture of user needs but also reduce the risk of costly changes later in the design process. With the insights gathered, designers can move confidently into the ideation and prototyping stages, building solutions grounded in real-world needs and behaviors.

Mastering research and discovery is essential for aspiring UI/UX designers, as it provides the tools to uncover user needs, make informed design decisions, and create products that people genuinely value.

Through these methods and tools, research and discovery reveal the true needs, behaviors, and motivations of users, setting a powerful foundation for creating experiences that genuinely resonate. For anyone entering the field, building strong research skills will provide an invaluable edge in creating thoughtful, user-centered designs.

04 Ideation and Concept Development

Once research and discovery have provided a solid understanding of the users, their needs, and their pain points, the next phase in the User-Centered Design (UCD) process is **ideation and concept development**. This phase is all about creativity, exploration, and collaboration, as designers start to brainstorm solutions that address the insights uncovered during research. Ideation and concept development are essential for generating a wide range of ideas, refining them, and identifying the ones with the most potential to deliver meaningful, user-centered experiences.

In this chapter, we'll explore the tools, techniques, and methodologies commonly used during ideation and concept development, detailing how they help designers translate user insights into tangible concepts that serve as the foundation for the design process.

The Purpose of Ideation and Concept Development

Ideation is a creative, divergent-thinking phase aimed at generating as many ideas as possible. Here, designers step back from the constraints of feasibility or usability testing and let their minds explore new possibilities. This stage encourages thinking beyond obvious solutions, allowing teams to unlock innovative approaches that may not have emerged otherwise. Concept development follows ideation, helping to refine and structure ideas into initial design concepts that can be evaluated, prototyped, and tested.

The ideation and concept development phase helps designers to:

- **Explore a range of solutions** without judgment, keeping options open before narrowing down.
- **Push past first ideas** to discover unexpected or novel solutions.
- **Collaborate and build on each other's ideas** for a richer pool of concepts.
- **Refine ideas into concrete concepts** that can be shared with stakeholders or taken into prototyping.

Key Techniques for Ideation and Concept Development

There are numerous ideation techniques available, each encouraging creative thinking and collaborative problem-solving in its own way.

Here, we cover some of the most popular and effective methods for the UCD process.

1. Brainstorming

Purpose: Brainstorming is a classic technique for generating a large volume of ideas in a short time. This method focuses on quantity over quality, allowing designers to freely propose ideas without immediate judgment or filtering.

Process: A facilitator poses a challenge or question based on research insights, and participants take turns suggesting ideas. Brainstorming sessions often use prompts like "How might we...?" to encourage open-ended thinking. Ideas are typically recorded on sticky notes or a shared digital space like Miro or FigJam.

Advantages:

- Encourages free thinking and minimizes self-censorship.
- Allows participants to build on each other's ideas in real-time.

Challenges:

- Can result in less structured ideas if not managed well.
- Dominant voices may overshadow quieter participants.

2. Mind Mapping

Purpose: Mind mapping helps organize ideas around a central theme or problem, creating a visual "map" of related thoughts, features, and possibilities. This technique is useful for breaking down complex problems into smaller, manageable parts.

Process: Designers start with a central idea (e.g., "improving onboarding") and branch out with related ideas, subtopics, or features. Mind mapping tools like MindMeister, Coggle, or a simple pen and paper can be used to create these visual diagrams.

Advantages:

- Visual structure helps clarify relationships between ideas.
- Great for brainstorming specific features or flows within a concept.

Challenges:

- May feel restrictive for those who prefer free-form ideation.
- Can become overly complex with too many branches or layers.

3. Crazy Eights

Purpose: Crazy Eights is a fast-paced ideation exercise designed to push participants to think creatively and avoid "safe" ideas. It's a sketching activity that generates a wide variety of visual ideas in a short time.

Process: Each participant folds a piece of paper into eight sections. In eight minutes, they draw eight quick sketches, one per section, exploring different ways to solve the design challenge. This technique is often used during design sprints to encourage divergent thinking.

Advantages:

- Fast, fun, and encourages out-of-the-box ideas.
- Helps overcome creative blocks by generating a large volume of ideas.

Challenges:

- Requires quick sketching skills; some participants may feel pressured.
- May not yield fully developed ideas but sparks new directions.

4. SCAMPER Technique

Purpose: SCAMPER (Substitute, Combine, Adapt, Modify, Put to another use, Eliminate, Reverse) is a method that encourages designers to look at existing ideas and rethink them in new ways. It's particularly helpful when building on ideas from competitive analysis or existing products.

Process: The SCAMPER framework guides participants through prompts, asking questions like "What could we substitute?" or "How could we adapt this idea for a different context?" By applying each SCAMPER step, designers can reimagine and transform current ideas, pushing beyond obvious solutions.

Advantages:

- Provides a structured framework to refine and innovate on existing ideas.
- Encourages creative modification and experimentation.

Challenges:

- Can be challenging if there are no clear existing ideas or products to build from.
- The structured nature may limit free-form thinking.

5. Storyboarding

Purpose: Storyboarding is a technique that visualizes the user's experience step-by-step, capturing how users might interact with the product and what their experience could look like over time. This method is particularly valuable for mapping user journeys and identifying potential pain points.

Process: Designers create a sequence of sketches or frames that represent key steps in a user's journey. Each frame includes a description of what's happening, the user's actions, and the anticipated emotional response. Storyboards can be created on paper, whiteboards, or digital tools like Storyboard That.

Advantages:

- Helps visualize the user experience and identifies areas for improvement.
- Provides a structured way to communicate the user journey to stakeholders.

Challenges:

- Requires time to create detailed sequences.
- May not capture every user scenario or edge case.

6. Role Playing

Purpose: Role playing, or "bodystorming," allows designers to physically act out a user scenario to better understand the context and emotional experience of the user. This technique brings empathy and a human touch to the ideation process.

Process: Participants adopt user personas and go through different interactions or experiences with the product, often improvising potential scenarios. Props or mockups can help make the scenario feel more realistic, encouraging participants to consider details they might otherwise overlook.

Advantages:

- Encourages empathy by putting designers "in the shoes" of the user.
- Brings out insights that may not emerge from theoretical discussions.

Challenges:

- Requires comfort with acting and improvisation.
- Not ideal for all design problems, especially those with complex interfaces.

Tools for Supporting Ideation and Concept Development

Several digital tools can facilitate ideation and concept development, especially when collaborating remotely or organizing a high volume of ideas.

- **Miro and FigJam:** These online whiteboards allow teams to brainstorm, mind map, and sketch together in real-time, making them ideal for group ideation sessions.
- **MindMeister and Coggle:** These tools are excellent for mind mapping, helping designers organize ideas and see connections between different concepts.
- **Adobe XD and Figma:** While primarily used for prototyping, these tools support early-stage concept sketches, wireframes, and layout explorations.
- **Stormboard and MURAL:** Both are visual collaboration tools that support brainstorming, sticky notes, and mind mapping, making them suitable for collaborative ideation.

Evaluating and Refining Concepts

After generating a wide range of ideas, the next step is to evaluate and refine them into concrete concepts that can be prototyped and tested. This stage combines elements of critical thinking and prioritization, helping teams move from raw ideas to structured design concepts.

1. Dot Voting

Purpose: Dot voting, also known as "dotmocracy," is a quick, democratic way to identify the most promising ideas after a brainstorming session. This method allows teams to prioritize ideas collectively.

Process: Participants review all generated ideas and place dots (stickers or digital icons) on their preferred ideas. The ideas with the most dots are selected for further refinement.

Advantages:

- Quick and effective for narrowing down large idea sets.
- Encourages participation and collective decision-making.

Challenges:

- Popular ideas may not always be the best solutions.
- Risk of "groupthink" if participants are influenced by each other's votes.

2. Impact-Effort Matrix

Purpose: The Impact-Effort Matrix helps teams evaluate ideas based on their potential impact and the effort required to implement them. This tool is particularly useful for prioritizing concepts in line with project goals and constraints.

Process: Designers plot ideas on a two-axis grid with "Impact" on one axis and "Effort" on the other. Ideas in the high-impact, low-effort quadrant are prioritized, while high-effort, low-impact ideas may be set aside.

Advantages:

- Provides a structured way to assess feasibility and impact.
- Helps focus on ideas that align with project resources and goals.

Challenges:

- Requires accurate estimates of impact and effort, which may be challenging.
- May exclude innovative ideas that require higher effort.

Why Ideation and Concept Development Matter in UCD

Ideation and concept development empower designers to explore a broad range of solutions before narrowing down to the most promising concepts. This phase encourages creativity, openness, and collaboration, ensuring that the design process isn't limited by initial assumptions or biases. By fostering a wide variety of ideas and refining them thoughtfully, designers are better equipped to develop user-centered solutions that address real needs in meaningful ways.

For aspiring UI/UX designers, honing these ideation skills is invaluable, as it provides the flexibility, creativity, and structure needed to transform user insights into impactful design solutions.

Through these techniques and tools, ideation and concept development bring user-centered insights to life, creating a foundation for design that is not only innovative but deeply connected to the users it serves.

05 Prototyping and Design

With a set of well-researched insights and promising ideas from the ideation phase, designers move into **prototyping and design**—the hands-on process of bringing ideas to life in tangible form. Prototyping allows designers to explore the look, feel, and functionality of their concepts, bridging the gap between ideas and user experiences. In the User-Centered Design (UCD) process, prototyping and design are iterative, constantly evolving based on user feedback and insights gained from testing.

This chapter covers the tools, techniques, and methodologies commonly used in prototyping and design, demonstrating how they help designers create, refine, and test their concepts to deliver meaningful user experiences.

The Purpose of Prototyping and Design

Prototyping and design allow designers to visualize and interact with their ideas, transforming abstract concepts into testable models. Prototypes enable teams to experiment with layouts, interactions, and navigation flows, giving users a preliminary feel for the product before moving to final design. This phase encourages designers to test assumptions, identify usability issues early, and gather critical user feedback, reducing the risk of major changes later in the development process.

Key benefits of prototyping and design include:

- **Testing design hypotheses** to validate functionality and usability.
- **Experimenting with interaction patterns and navigation flows** to enhance usability.
- **Gaining user feedback** in a realistic context before full development.
- **Refining visual elements** like colors, typography, and layout to create an appealing, consistent experience.

Types of Prototypes

Different stages of the design process call for different types of prototypes, each suited to specific objectives and levels of fidelity.

1. **Low-Fidelity Prototypes**
   Low-fidelity prototypes are rough, simplified representations of the

product, typically focusing on layout and structure rather than visual details. These prototypes are often created as sketches or wireframes to test basic functionality and flow.

- o **Purpose:** Quickly explore layout options, gather early feedback on structure, and test basic interactions.
- o **Tools:** Sketching, paper prototypes, whiteboards, or basic digital wireframing tools like Balsamiq.

2. **Mid-Fidelity Prototypes**

Mid-fidelity prototypes add a layer of functionality and interactivity, allowing users to navigate through different screens and experience core interactions. They help designers validate user flows and structural elements without committing to final visuals.

- o **Purpose:** Test navigation and functionality in greater detail; start incorporating some interaction elements.
- o **Tools:** Digital prototyping tools like Figma, Sketch, or Adobe XD with basic interactive elements.

3. **High-Fidelity Prototypes**

High-fidelity prototypes are closer to the final product, incorporating detailed visuals, branding, and realistic interactions. These prototypes are ideal for usability testing, as they provide a more accurate experience of the final design.

- o **Purpose:** Gather in-depth feedback on both functionality and aesthetics; simulate a near-final experience.
- o **Tools:** Advanced digital prototyping tools like Figma, Adobe XD, or Axure with robust interactive elements, animations, and transitions.

4. **Interactive and Functional Prototypes**

Interactive prototypes simulate the product's full functionality, often with advanced animations, transitions, and user flows. While they require more effort to create, they are invaluable for testing complex interactions and demonstrating the product to stakeholders.

- o **Purpose:** Test complex interactions and transitions; demonstrate the product vision to stakeholders.
- o **Tools:** InVision, Principle, ProtoPie, or Framer, which offer sophisticated interactive capabilities.

Key Prototyping Techniques in User-Centered Design

Prototyping techniques range from quick sketches to fully interactive digital models, and each has its own role in the design process.

1. Sketching and Paper Prototyping

Purpose: Sketching and paper prototyping offer a quick, low-cost way to explore ideas and test layouts, allowing designers to brainstorm and iterate without getting bogged down in details.

Process: Designers create hand-drawn sketches or paper cutouts of screens, showing layouts and basic navigation. These can be tested by walking users through tasks and observing how they interact with the screens. Feedback is collected to refine ideas before committing to digital designs.

Advantages:

- Rapid and inexpensive; ideal for early ideation and layout exploration.
- Encourages open-ended, flexible experimentation.

Challenges:

- Limited interactivity; may not fully convey flow and functionality.
- Best suited for early-stage testing rather than detailed user feedback.

2. Wireframing

Purpose: Wireframing is the process of creating skeletal layouts for each screen, defining structure and hierarchy without focusing on detailed visuals. Wireframes provide a blueprint for the design, showing where content, navigation, and functionality will be placed.

Process: Designers use digital wireframing tools to create layouts, identifying where buttons, images, text, and navigation elements will appear on each screen. Wireframes are shared with stakeholders and often tested with users to gather feedback on structure and flow.

Advantages:

- Helps designers focus on layout and user flow without visual distractions.
- Provides a clear structural framework for moving into higher fidelity designs.

Challenges:

- Limited visual detail; some users may struggle to imagine the final design.
- May need to be redone as high-fidelity prototypes in later stages.

3. Digital Prototyping

Purpose: Digital prototyping involves creating interactive models of the design using software that allows users to click through and experience basic interactions. These prototypes range from mid- to high-fidelity, depending on the level of detail and realism needed.

Process: Using tools like Figma, Adobe XD, or InVision, designers add interactions, transitions, and clickable areas to their designs, allowing users to navigate through flows and experience the product. Digital prototypes can simulate real user interactions and help uncover usability issues in navigation and functionality.

Advantages:

- Provides realistic interactions, enhancing usability testing.
- Easy to share with stakeholders and gather feedback remotely.

Challenges:

- Requires more time and effort to create, especially at higher fidelity.
- Complex interactions may be challenging to fully replicate.

4. Clickable Prototypes

Purpose: Clickable prototypes allow users to interact with key screens, testing flows and navigation without full functionality. This approach is ideal for testing user paths and identifying any friction points in the journey.

Process: Designers identify key screens and user actions, linking screens together with basic interactions. Clickable prototypes are often created at mid-fidelity to test user flows and initial design assumptions.

Advantages:

- Provides users with a sense of interaction and navigation flow.
- Easy to build and update for quick feedback cycles.

Challenges:

- Limited functionality; may not capture every interaction detail.
- Requires a balance of simplicity and functionality.

5. High-Fidelity Interactive Prototyping

Purpose: High-fidelity interactive prototypes replicate the final design as closely as possible, including visual details, animations, and complex interactions. These prototypes are used to validate aesthetics and test intricate flows before full development.

Process: Designers use tools like Framer or ProtoPie to incorporate high-fidelity visuals and advanced interactions, simulating the final experience. These prototypes are ideal for in-depth usability testing and stakeholder presentations.

Advantages:

- Provides an accurate representation of the final product.
- Allows detailed testing of complex interactions and visual effects.

Challenges:

- High time investment; best suited for later stages of design.
- May require specialized tools and skills for advanced interactions.

Tools for Prototyping and Design

Modern prototyping tools allow designers to create interactive, realistic prototypes that can be shared and tested with ease. Here are some commonly used tools in the UCD process:

- **Figma:** A collaborative tool for designing interfaces and prototyping, Figma allows designers to create clickable prototypes, apply interactions, and collaborate in real time.
- **Adobe XD:** Known for its robust prototyping features, Adobe XD supports interactions, transitions, and even voice-based prototyping.
- **Sketch + InVision:** Designers often pair Sketch for UI design with InVision for prototyping, as InVision allows for linking screens and creating interactive flows.

- **Axure:** Known for advanced prototyping capabilities, Axure is ideal for creating complex, data-driven interactions in high-fidelity prototypes.
- **Framer and ProtoPie:** These tools support high-fidelity, interactive prototypes with sophisticated animations and transitions, ideal for presenting polished designs.

Iterative Design and Refinement

Prototyping is an iterative process, often involving cycles of design, testing, feedback, and refinement. With each round of testing, prototypes are adjusted to resolve usability issues, address user feedback, and move closer to the final design. This approach aligns with the user-centered methodology, where ongoing user input helps guide the design in real-time, ensuring it stays aligned with user needs and expectations.

1. Usability Testing

Purpose: Usability testing is the process of observing real users as they interact with a prototype, allowing designers to identify and resolve any issues in navigation, layout, or interaction. Usability tests are crucial for gathering insights on how well the prototype performs and where users encounter friction.

Process: Designers create tasks that guide users through typical interactions, observing where they succeed or encounter challenges. Feedback is documented, analyzed, and used to inform adjustments in the next iteration.

Advantages:

- Provides direct insights into user behavior and design performance.
- Allows designers to identify usability issues early, reducing costly changes.

Challenges:

- Requires preparation and recruitment of representative users.
- May yield subjective feedback that needs careful interpretation.

2. Feedback Gathering and Iteration

Purpose: Feedback gathering is essential throughout prototyping, ensuring that the design evolves with input from users, stakeholders, and team members.

Process: Designers gather feedback from usability tests, stakeholder reviews, or team critiques, documenting key points and prioritizing issues based on impact and feasibility. Each feedback cycle informs adjustments in the prototype, moving it closer to the final design.

Advantages:

- Encourages a user-centered approach, ensuring designs meet real needs.
- Facilitates collaboration and alignment with stakeholders and team members.

Challenges:

- Can require multiple cycles of feedback, which may extend timelines.
- Feedback needs to be carefully balanced with project constraints.

Why Prototyping and Design Matter in UCD

Prototyping and design allow designers to explore ideas, test assumptions, and create user-centered experiences that resonate with people. By using iterative prototyping, designers can catch potential issues early, refine details based on feedback, and ensure that the final product is not only functional but delightful to use. This phase of the UCD process is where ideas become experiences, ensuring that design decisions are always rooted in user needs and real-world context.

For those entering the field, developing strong prototyping skills and an iterative mindset is invaluable, enabling you to create thoughtful, effective designs that are truly centered around the user.

Through careful prototyping and iterative design, user-centered design transforms insights into impactful, interactive experiences, helping create products that users will value and enjoy.

06 User Testing and Evaluation

User testing and evaluation are the linchpins of the User-Centered Design (UCD) process. This phase is where designs meet reality, as users interact with prototypes, providing feedback that guides refinement and helps identify any usability issues. The purpose of user testing is to validate the design with real users, ensuring that it's intuitive, functional, and enjoyable before final development. It's the process of listening, observing, and learning from users as they interact with your design, creating a feedback loop that drives iterative improvement.

In this chapter, we'll explore the tools, techniques, and methodologies commonly used in user testing and evaluation, each serving a unique purpose in gathering insights that shape the final product.

The Purpose of User Testing and Evaluation

User testing and evaluation help designers uncover how users perceive, understand, and navigate through the product. By putting designs in the hands of real users, designers can identify points of friction, clarify assumptions, and fine-tune elements to ensure a seamless experience. User testing also ensures that the design meets both functional and emotional goals, offering insights into areas where users might struggle or feel frustrated.

The key benefits of user testing and evaluation include:

- **Validating design decisions** to ensure they align with user needs.
- **Identifying usability issues** that may not have been apparent during prototyping.
- **Collecting feedback** on layout, navigation, and interaction design.
- **Ensuring accessibility and inclusivity** by evaluating the experience across diverse user groups.

Types of User Testing

User testing can take various forms, each suited to different stages of the design process and different types of feedback.

1. **Usability Testing**
   Usability testing focuses on assessing how easy and efficient the design is for users to navigate and complete tasks. It's a

foundational testing method in UCD, helping designers evaluate the intuitiveness of the interface and detect any obstacles.

- **Purpose:** Test the ease of use and functionality of the design; identify pain points and inefficiencies in navigation.
- **Tools:** UserTesting, Lookback, Maze, or in-person testing with recording software like QuickTime or Zoom.

2. **A/B Testing**

A/B testing is a method of comparing two variations of a design element to see which performs better in achieving a specific goal, such as clicks, engagement, or conversions. This method is useful for evaluating minor changes and optimizing user flows.

- **Purpose:** Test different design variations to determine which version yields better user engagement or task success.
- **Tools:** Google Optimize, Optimizely, and Adobe Target.

3. **Preference Testing**

Preference testing allows users to compare multiple design options and choose the one they prefer. This technique helps designers understand user preferences on visual elements like color schemes, typography, and layout.

- **Purpose:** Collect subjective feedback on visual or aesthetic aspects; gauge user preferences for different design styles.
- **Tools:** UsabilityHub, Pollfish, and Google Forms for simplified polling.

4. **Surveys and Questionnaires**

Surveys are a versatile tool for gathering quantitative and qualitative feedback from a larger audience, often used after usability testing to get general impressions about the experience.

- **Purpose:** Gather feedback on user satisfaction, ease of use, and general design impressions from a broader sample.

- Tools: SurveyMonkey, Google Forms, and Typeform.
5. **Eye Tracking and Heat Mapping**

   Eye tracking and heat mapping reveal where users are focusing on the screen, providing insights into visual hierarchy, layout effectiveness, and areas of interest. These methods help designers optimize layouts and ensure that important elements capture user attention.

   - **Purpose:** Understand where users are looking and how they visually navigate a page; improve placement of key elements.
   - **Tools:** Eye-tracking hardware like Tobii or online tools like Hotjar (for heat maps).

6. **Remote Usability Testing**

   Remote usability testing allows users to test the design from their own environment, providing insights into real-world usage. This is particularly valuable for reaching a geographically dispersed audience or collecting feedback in natural settings.

   - **Purpose:** Gather usability feedback from a diverse user group; observe user interactions remotely.
   - **Tools:** UserTesting, Lookback, Maze, and Zoom.

Key Techniques for User Testing in UCD

User testing is most effective when it combines structured observation, open feedback, and detailed analysis. Here are some of the most widely used techniques in UCD testing.

1. Think-Aloud Protocol

Purpose: The think-aloud protocol encourages users to verbalize their thoughts, feelings, and decisions as they interact with the design. This technique provides insights into users' mental processes, helping designers understand why they make certain choices.

Process: Users are asked to speak out loud about what they are doing, what they are looking at, and any difficulties they encounter. Designers observe and document the process, noting any moments of confusion or hesitation.

Advantages:

- Provides insights into user expectations and mental models.
- Helps identify areas where the design may be confusing or unclear.

Challenges:

- Some users may find it difficult to verbalize their thoughts naturally.
- Requires skilled facilitators to encourage users without leading them.

2. Task Analysis

Purpose: Task analysis involves assigning specific tasks for users to complete within the prototype. By observing how users approach each task, designers can pinpoint friction points and see if the design supports intuitive interactions.

Process: Users are given a set of tasks that represent common actions or goals within the product. Designers observe users' actions, noting where they encounter challenges or inefficiencies in completing tasks.

Advantages:

- Allows for precise, task-specific feedback.
- Useful for testing key interactions and navigation flows.

Challenges:

- Tasks need to be well-defined to yield relevant feedback.
- May not capture unexpected user behaviors or use cases.

3. Card Sorting

Purpose: Card sorting helps designers understand how users group information, making it particularly useful for navigation and information architecture design. By asking users to organize topics into categories, designers can identify intuitive labeling and organizational structures.

Process: Users are given "cards" (physical or digital) representing content or functionality and asked to organize them into categories. Open card sorting lets users create their own categories, while closed card sorting provides predefined categories.

Advantages:

- Reveals how users interpret and structure content.
- Guides the creation of a logical and intuitive information hierarchy.

Challenges:

- Results may vary based on user familiarity with the subject.
- Limited to structuring content, without insights on interaction.

4. First-Click Testing

Purpose: First-click testing evaluates whether users' first clicks on the interface lead them closer to their goal. This technique is especially valuable for testing navigation, as the first click is often a predictor of task success.

Process: Users are asked to complete a task, and designers observe their first click or tap. If the first click leads users toward their goal, the navigation is likely intuitive; if not, it may require revision.

Advantages:

- Provides quick, actionable insights on navigation and information hierarchy.
- Predicts the success rate for users completing tasks.

Challenges:

- Focuses only on initial navigation, without assessing complete task flows.
- Limited insights on design aesthetics or long-term user engagement.

5. Guerrilla Testing

Purpose: Guerrilla testing is a low-cost, informal approach to usability testing that involves gathering quick feedback from users in public or semi-public settings. This method is particularly useful for early-stage testing or rapid feedback cycles.

Process: Designers approach users in casual settings (e.g., coffee shops or libraries) and ask them to interact with the prototype, often offering small incentives like coffee or a gift card. Feedback is collected informally to gauge initial reactions.

Advantages:

- Cost-effective and quick; useful for early-stage feedback.
- Minimal planning and setup required.

Challenges:

- Limited depth and often lacks demographic targeting.
- May not capture detailed usability issues or long-term engagement.

6. Heuristic Evaluation

Purpose: Heuristic evaluation involves usability experts evaluating the design against established usability principles, or heuristics, such as Jakob Nielsen's 10 usability heuristics. This approach highlights potential issues without the need for user testing.

Process: A group of usability experts individually evaluates the prototype, documenting any violations of usability principles. Results are compiled, and designers address issues based on priority.

Advantages:

- Provides expert-driven insights quickly and cost-effectively.
- Useful for identifying common usability problems early.

Challenges:

- Relies on expert judgment, which may differ from actual user behavior.
- Limited perspective; may miss issues that real users encounter.

Tools for User Testing and Evaluation

User testing tools streamline the process of collecting, analyzing, and sharing user feedback. Below are some of the most commonly used tools in the UCD process:

- **UserTesting:** A platform for remote usability testing that provides video recordings of users as they interact with the prototype, along with tools for task creation and analysis.
- **Lookback:** A remote testing tool that enables designers to observe users live or through recordings, offering the ability to annotate and analyze sessions.
- **Maze:** An intuitive, data-driven testing tool that supports usability testing, surveys, and first-click testing, allowing for rapid feedback cycles.
- **Hotjar:** Provides heat maps, click tracking, and session recordings, making it easy to see where users focus their attention and identify navigation patterns.
- **Optimal Workshop:** A suite of tools for card sorting, tree testing, and first-click testing, helping designers refine information architecture and navigation.

Analyzing and Synthesizing User Testing Results

Once testing is complete, the next step is to analyze and synthesize the findings into actionable insights that guide design adjustments.

1. Affinity Diagramming

Purpose: Affinity diagramming organizes feedback into categories, helping designers identify patterns and prioritize issues. This approach is particularly helpful when working with qualitative feedback from interviews or usability tests.

Process: Designers review all feedback, grouping similar observations and insights on a visual board. Patterns are then analyzed, revealing common themes or issues that need attention.

Advantages:

- Provides a clear visual representation of user feedback.
- Encourages collaborative review of test results.

Challenges:

- Time-consuming with large amounts of data.
- Requires skill to effectively categorize and interpret data.

2. Usability Metrics Analysis

Purpose: Quantitative metrics such as task completion rate, time on task, and error rate provide objective data on usability. These metrics help designers assess usability performance and identify any areas needing improvement.

Process: Designers track and calculate usability metrics during testing sessions. The results are then analyzed, with focus on tasks with high error rates or low completion rates.

Advantages:

- Provides objective data to measure usability.
- Allows for benchmarking across iterations.

Challenges:

- Quantitative data may lack context for understanding issues.
- Limited scope for evaluating subjective experience.

Why User Testing and Evaluation Matter in UCD

User testing and evaluation are essential for validating the design, refining details, and building a product that genuinely meets user needs. Through user testing, designers gain a firsthand look at how people interact with the product, identifying opportunities to enhance usability, accessibility, and overall satisfaction. This phase grounds design decisions in real-world feedback, ensuring that the final product is effective, intuitive, and aligned with user expectations.

For aspiring UI/UX designers, developing skills in user testing and evaluation is invaluable, enabling you to create designs that are both user-friendly and responsive to feedback.

By embracing a thorough user testing and evaluation process, designers can confidently move forward, knowing that their product is guided by user insights, refined by feedback, and designed to make a positive impact in users' lives.

07 Design Sprints

Design Sprints are a fast-paced, structured approach to solving big design challenges in a condensed time frame, often five days or less. Originally developed by Google Ventures, the Design Sprint framework is now widely adopted across industries as a way to test ideas quickly, gather user feedback, and minimize the risks of lengthy product development cycles. Design Sprints are ideal for teams looking to rapidly validate concepts, refine user-centered designs, or make critical decisions on product direction.

This chapter explores the Google Ventures (GV) Design Sprint methodology, the tools and techniques used at each stage, and how designers can adapt the sprint format to fit their unique design processes and company cultures.

The Purpose of Design Sprints

The primary goal of a Design Sprint is to take an idea from concept to user-validated prototype in a matter of days. By compressing the design and development process into a focused sprint, teams can quickly test assumptions, explore potential solutions, and gather user feedback before investing in full-scale development. Design Sprints are particularly useful for tackling high-stakes design challenges, testing new features, or aligning cross-functional teams on a shared vision.

Key benefits of Design Sprints include:

- **Rapid validation of ideas** without extensive resource commitments.
- **Minimized risk** by testing concepts before development.
- **Enhanced team alignment** through a structured, collaborative process.
- **User-centered design focus** by including user feedback and testing within the sprint.

The Google Ventures (GV) Design Sprint: A Five-Day Framework

The Google Ventures Design Sprint condenses the design process into a structured five-day format, with each day dedicated to a specific stage of the design journey. Let's explore the stages, key activities, and tools used in each day of a traditional GV Design Sprint.

Day 1: Understand and Define

On the first day, the goal is to understand the problem space, align on sprint objectives, and define a clear focus for the week. This involves gathering background information, identifying user needs, and setting a clear sprint goal.

- **Key Activities:**
    - **Map the User Journey:** Create a high-level map of the user journey, focusing on key steps and pain points.
    - **Define the Sprint Challenge:** Outline the specific problem or opportunity the team will address during the sprint.
    - **Expert Interviews:** Gather insights from stakeholders, industry experts, or team members with relevant knowledge.
- **Tools:**
    - **Miro or MURAL:** Online whiteboards for mapping and brainstorming.
    - **Post-it Notes and Sharpies:** Essential for brainstorming and organizing ideas in physical settings.
    - **Persona Profiles:** Use pre-existing user personas or empathy maps to guide understanding of user needs.

Day 2: Sketch Solutions

The second day is all about ideation and solution exploration. The goal is to generate a wide range of potential solutions and explore creative approaches to solving the challenge.

- **Key Activities:**
  - Lightning Demos: Review existing solutions or products for inspiration, focusing on what works well.
  - **Crazy Eights:** A rapid sketching exercise where participants sketch eight variations of a solution in eight minutes.
  - **Solution Sketching:** Each participant creates a detailed sketch of their top solution idea, focusing on clarity and feasibility.
- **Tools:**
  - **Paper and Pens:** For sketching and iterating on ideas.
  - **FigJam or Miro:** For digital sketching and sharing ideas in remote settings.
  - **Image and Inspiration Boards:** Collect screenshots or visuals from competitive products to inspire solution ideas.

Day 3: Decide and Storyboard

On the third day, the team evaluates the solutions generated on Day 2, decides on the best concept to prototype, and creates a storyboard that outlines the user experience step-by-step.

- **Key Activities:**
  - **Dot Voting:** A quick voting method where team members place dots on preferred ideas, helping identify the strongest concepts.

- Decision-Making: A designated "Decider" (usually a team leader) makes the final choice on which solution to prototype.
  - Storyboard: Create a visual storyboard that maps out each step in the user journey, ensuring clarity on the prototype's flow.
- **Tools:**
  - **Storyboard Templates:** Templates in tools like Miro or Sketch for organizing the flow of the chosen solution.
  - **Dot Stickers or Digital Voting:** For voting on ideas, both in-person and digitally.
  - **Whiteboards or Digital Canvases:** For creating storyboards that can be easily referenced during prototyping.

Day 4: Prototype

On the fourth day, the team builds a high-fidelity prototype based on the storyboard. This prototype should be realistic enough to gather meaningful feedback but does not need full functionality.

- **Key Activities:**
  - **Assign Roles:** Team members take on roles (e.g., designer, writer, tester) to streamline the prototyping process.
  - **Build the Prototype:** Using tools like Figma, Sketch, or Adobe XD, designers create an interactive prototype based on the storyboard.

- - Mock Data and Content: Add realistic data, images, and copy to give the prototype authenticity and context.
- Tools:
  - Figma or Adobe XD: For designing interactive, clickable prototypes.
  - InVision: To add interactions and share prototypes for testing.
  - Photoshop and Illustrator: For creating visual assets and editing images to enhance the prototype.

Day 5: Test and Learn

The final day of the sprint is dedicated to user testing. Designers conduct usability tests with real users, gather feedback, and document insights. This step allows the team to learn which aspects of the prototype work well and where adjustments are needed.

- Key Activities:
  - User Testing Sessions: Schedule 5–7 users for one-on-one testing sessions, asking them to complete specific tasks within the prototype.
  - Observation and Note-Taking: Record users' actions and reactions, noting any pain points or confusion.
  - Debrief and Synthesize Feedback: Analyze user feedback and discuss next steps, determining what to keep, change, or explore further.

- **Tools:**
  - ○ **UserTesting or Lookback:** For remote testing sessions and capturing user feedback.
  - ○ **Maze or UsabilityHub:** For remote, self-guided usability testing.
  - ○ **Miro or Sticky Notes:** To categorize feedback, identify patterns, and prioritize issues for the next iteration.

Adapting the GV Design Sprint Methodology

While the five-day GV Design Sprint framework is effective, it's not always feasible for every organization or project. Many companies adapt the sprint format to fit their specific needs, resources, and timelines. Here are some ways designers can customize the Google Design Sprint methodology to align with their own processes and company culture.

1. Shorter Sprints (2–3 Days)

For teams with limited time, condensing the sprint into two or three days can still provide valuable insights. Shorter sprints typically involve selecting the highest-impact activities, such as ideation, prototyping, and a condensed user testing phase.

- **Tips for Shorter Sprints:**
  - ○ Skip the storyboard and go straight to prototyping, focusing on essential interactions.
  - ○ Select a smaller scope for testing, perhaps focusing on a single user flow or feature.

2. Flexible Scheduling

Some teams prefer to spread out the sprint over several weeks, dedicating a few hours each day to the sprint activities. This approach allows for a more flexible schedule that accommodates other responsibilities and is particularly useful for teams with dispersed members or limited availability.

- **Tips for Flexible Sprints:**
    - Schedule touchpoints with stakeholders at key stages (e.g., after prototyping and before testing).
    - Use asynchronous collaboration tools like Slack and shared boards in Miro to keep momentum going.

3. Virtual Design Sprints

For remote teams, running a virtual Design Sprint requires adapting activities for digital collaboration. Many tools support real-time collaboration, making it possible to conduct ideation, prototyping, and testing entirely online.

- **Tips for Virtual Sprints:**
    - Use online whiteboards like Miro or MURAL for brainstorming, storyboarding, and voting.
    - Leverage video conferencing for real-time discussions, ideation, and debriefs.
    - Use cloud-based design tools (e.g., Figma or Adobe XD) for seamless, collaborative prototyping.

4. Adapting to Team Culture

Design Sprints can also be tailored to fit a team's culture and workflow preferences. For example, teams that value open collaboration may involve a larger group for brainstorming, while teams with a top-down decision-making structure may assign more control to a designated "Decider."

- **Tips for Adapting to Culture:**
    - Emphasize transparency and communication if collaboration is highly valued.
    - Allow flexibility in decision-making by using voting rounds or feedback sessions that fit the company's style.
    - Align sprint goals with company objectives and metrics to ensure relevance.

Tools for Supporting Design Sprints

Design Sprints rely on a range of digital tools to facilitate brainstorming, prototyping, and testing. Here are some commonly used tools that enhance the Design Sprint experience:

- **Miro and MURAL:** These online whiteboards are perfect for brainstorming, voting, storyboarding, and capturing feedback, making them essential for remote or in-person sprints.
- **Figma, Sketch, and Adobe XD:** Design tools that support collaborative prototyping, helping teams quickly build and iterate on ideas.

- **User Testing and Lookback:** Tools for remote user testing that allow teams to observe user interactions, collect feedback, and analyze usability insights.
- **Slack and Zoom:** Communication tools that help teams coordinate during sprints, share updates, and stay connected across locations.

Why Design Sprints Matter in UCD

Design Sprints provide a powerful framework for rapid experimentation, collaboration, and validation, making them an invaluable tool in User-Centered Design. By condensing the design process into an intense, focused sprint, teams can move quickly from problem to solution, gathering insights that inform the larger design and development strategy. Design Sprints bring together designers, stakeholders, and users in a structured way, ensuring that each voice contributes to the final product's success.

For aspiring UI/UX designers, mastering Design Sprints not only sharpens problem-solving skills but also fosters adaptability, collaboration, and user empathy, all of which are essential in user-centered design.

Through their focus on fast-paced experimentation and real user feedback, Design Sprints help turn user insights into validated solutions, bringing user-centered design to life in a structured, impactful way.

08 Design Language Systems (DLS)

A Design Language System (DLS) is a collection of reusable components, design standards, and guidelines that work together to create a cohesive and recognizable experience across a product or brand. By defining a common "language" for visual, interaction, and experiential design, a DLS helps unify the work of designers, developers, and stakeholders, ensuring consistency, efficiency, and a strong brand identity. For companies with multiple digital products or large, cross-functional teams, a DLS is essential for maintaining a unified look and feel across all touchpoints.

In this chapter, we'll explore the components, benefits, and role of Design Language Systems in the User-Centered Design (UCD) process. We'll also look at notable DLS examples from prominent companies and discuss how designers can create and implement a DLS that fits their brand and user needs.

What is a Design Language System?

A Design Language System is a centralized repository of design principles, patterns, and components that guide how a brand's products look, feel, and function. A DLS often includes visual elements (such as typography, color schemes, and iconography), interaction patterns (buttons, forms, navigation elements), and sometimes even voice and tone guidelines for content. By consolidating these elements, a DLS ensures that each product is visually cohesive, accessible, and aligned with the brand's identity.

The main components of a typical DLS include:

- **Design Principles:** Foundational rules that guide decision-making, ensuring all design elements align with the brand's values and user goals.
- **Visual Style Guide:** A set of guidelines covering color palettes, typography, iconography, and imagery that creates a consistent aesthetic.
- **Component Library:** Reusable UI components (buttons, forms, modals, cards) that are pre-designed and pre-coded for ease of use.
- **Interaction Patterns:** Guidelines for behavior, such as hover states, button animations, loading indicators, and transitions, to create intuitive user experiences.
- **Accessibility Standards:** Ensuring that all components and patterns meet accessibility standards, making the product inclusive for all users.

The Importance of Design Language Systems in UCD

For companies focusing on user-centered design, a DLS provides a structure that empowers teams to create products that are both visually cohesive and highly usable. A well-defined DLS allows designers and developers to move quickly without sacrificing consistency, enabling them to focus on creating user-centered solutions rather than constantly reinventing UI elements.

Key benefits of a Design Language System in UCD include:

1. **Consistency Across Products**
   A DLS ensures that every product and feature aligns visually and functionally with the brand's identity, creating a cohesive experience that feels familiar to users across all touchpoints. Consistency builds trust, improves usability, and reduces the cognitive load on users who interact with multiple products within the brand ecosystem.
2. **Efficiency and Scalability**
   With a DLS, designers and developers have access to a library of pre-designed, reusable components. This not only accelerates the design and development process but also makes it easier to scale new products and features without starting from scratch.
3. **Improved Collaboration**
   A DLS provides a shared language and set of standards that align cross-functional teams on design goals and guidelines. Designers, developers, and product managers can work more

collaboratively, using the DLS as a reference point to make decisions quickly and reduce miscommunication.

4. **Focus on User Needs**

   By taking care of design consistency and standards, a DLS allows teams to focus their time and energy on understanding and addressing user needs. Designers can spend more time on research, prototyping, and user testing rather than on repetitive design tasks.

5. **Enhanced Accessibility**

   When accessibility is built into the components and guidelines of a DLS, all products benefit. Accessibility standards, such as color contrast, screen reader support, and keyboard navigation, become part of every design and development decision, ensuring inclusivity is embedded in the system.

Notable Design Language Systems from Prominent Companies

Several companies have set the standard for effective Design Language Systems, creating systems that are widely recognized and used as benchmarks within the design industry. Here are a few notable examples of DLS from leading brands:

1. Material Design by Google (https://m3.material.io/)

Material Design is Google's comprehensive design system, providing guidelines for colors, typography, layout, and even motion. Initially developed to unify Google's diverse suite of products, Material Design is now open-source and widely used by designers and developers outside

Google. Its foundation is built on principles like "bold, graphic, intentional" and "motion provides meaning," which guide Google's design philosophy [Google, 2014].

- **Highlights:**
    - Emphasis on realistic, tactile elements and shadows to create a sense of depth.
    - Consistent, layered navigation and interaction patterns.
    - Extensive documentation and design guidelines available for web and mobile platforms.

2. Carbon by IBM (https://carbondesignsystem.com/)

IBM's Carbon Design System was created to ensure a unified experience across the company's wide-ranging product portfolio. Carbon is built on a modular framework, allowing IBM's teams to create consistent, accessible designs while also being flexible enough to accommodate unique needs.

- **Highlights:**
    - Accessibility is a core focus, with guidelines for contrast, text size, and ARIA attributes.
    - Emphasis on modular, customizable components that are easily scalable.
    - Extensive visual and content guidelines that capture IBM's brand identity and tone.

3. Polaris by Shopify (https://polaris.shopify.com/)

Polaris is Shopify's Design Language System, designed to help third-party developers create experiences that feel native to the Shopify platform. Polaris includes guidelines for everything from UI components to content tone, with a strong focus on helping merchants create a consistent and user-friendly e-commerce experience.

- **Highlights:**
    - Emphasis on a merchant-first approach, with user empathy built into the design principles.
    - Guidelines for both UI and UX writing, ensuring consistency in communication style.
    - Comprehensive documentation and component library for Shopify's unique e-commerce needs.

4. Fluent by Microsoft (https://fluent2.microsoft.design/)

Fluent Design is Microsoft's DLS, providing design and interaction patterns for web, Windows, and mobile applications. Fluent focuses on creating a seamless experience across Microsoft's diverse products and platforms, incorporating principles like light, depth, motion, and material.

- **Highlights:**
    - A focus on fluid, responsive layouts and adaptable components for different screen sizes.

- Guidelines for multi-platform consistency, ensuring a cohesive experience across Windows, iOS, Android, and web.
- Extensive resources for incorporating motion, depth, and texture to enhance user interaction.

5. Atlassian Design System (https://atlassian.design/)

Atlassian's Design System supports a suite of products like Jira, Confluence, and Trello. Known for its user-first approach, the Atlassian Design System emphasizes ease of use and functional consistency across a suite of complex, collaborative tools.

- **Highlights:**
    - A detailed content style guide focused on clear, user-friendly language.
    - Modular components tailored to Atlassian's collaborative, task-oriented tools.
    - Emphasis on inclusive design with resources for accessibility and inclusivity.

Creating and Implementing a Design Language System

For companies looking to create a DLS, it's essential to start with a clear understanding of the brand's goals, user needs, and existing design principles. A successful DLS should be flexible enough to evolve with the product but structured enough to maintain consistency across all touchpoints. Here are some key steps and best practices for creating and implementing a DLS:

1. Define the Design Principles

Design principles are the foundation of any DLS, serving as the core values that guide decision-making. These principles should reflect the brand's personality and align with user expectations. For instance, if the brand values accessibility, one principle could be "Design for Everyone," ensuring that inclusivity is a core consideration.

2. Build a Component Library

A robust component library includes all the UI elements that designers and developers will need, from buttons and forms to modals and navigation bars. Each component should have documentation on usage guidelines, accessibility standards, and code snippets to ensure easy implementation.

- **Tip:** Start with core elements (e.g., buttons, typography, color palette) and expand as the design needs grow. Ensure that each component is tested for usability and accessibility before adding it to the library.

3. Document Interaction Patterns

Define guidelines for interactions such as animations, hover states, transitions, and gestures. Interaction patterns create consistency in user experience and make it easier for users to learn how to navigate the product.

- **Tip:** For each interaction pattern, include examples and usage scenarios to help designers and developers understand when and how to apply them.

4. Establish Accessibility Standards

Accessibility should be an integral part of the DLS, ensuring that all components are designed to meet WCAG standards. This includes considerations for color contrast, text size, keyboard navigation, and screen reader compatibility.

- **Tip:** Regularly test components with accessibility tools (e.g., Axe, Lighthouse) to ensure compliance and inclusivity.

5. Create Clear and Accessible Documentation

Documentation is the heart of a DLS, providing guidance on everything from component usage to design rationale. Comprehensive, accessible documentation ensures that all teams, regardless of location or role, can use the DLS effectively.

- **Tip:** Use tools like Storybook or Zeroheight to create interactive, easy-to-navigate documentation that can be updated as the DLS evolves.

Adapting a DLS to Fit Your Company Culture

Every organization has unique workflows, values, and user needs, so adapting a DLS to fit your company culture is essential. For some teams, flexibility and customization may be priorities, while others may prioritize strict adherence to standards. Here are a few ways to tailor a DLS to your team:

1. **Align DLS Principles with Company Values:** If your company emphasizes innovation, your DLS might allow more flexibility for experimentation, incorporating guidelines for trying new interactions or visuals. If accessibility is a top priority, ensure it's embedded in every aspect of the DLS.

2. **Gather Continuous Feedback:** Keep lines of communication open with designers and developers to refine and improve the DLS based on their needs. Feedback loops help identify areas for improvement and allow for a more adaptable, user-centered system.

3. **Encourage Contributions:** Allow team members to contribute components or suggest updates to the DLS. This fosters a sense of ownership and ensures the system evolves with the company's needs.

4. **Provide Flexibility for Innovation:** While consistency is essential, allow room for designers to push boundaries when appropriate. A flexible DLS might have "core" components that must be used, alongside "flexible" components that allow for experimentation.

Why Design Language Systems Matter in UCD

A Design Language System is invaluable in User-Centered Design because it provides a stable foundation that prioritizes consistency, efficiency, and usability. For designers, developers, and stakeholders, a DLS simplifies the creation of cohesive, intuitive products, freeing up time and resources to focus on user needs rather than design basics. By embedding best practices, accessibility, and brand identity into every element, a DLS ensures that all products are designed with the user in mind.

Through a thoughtfully developed DLS, companies create a user-centered experience that's as visually compelling as it is functional, ensuring that each product aligns with brand values and delivers an exceptional experience for users.

09 Guiding Design Principles

Design principles are foundational guidelines that inform and inspire design decisions, serving as a "north star" for creating cohesive, purposeful user experiences. More than a list of best practices, design principles reflect a brand's values, user needs, and strategic goals, guiding designers to make choices that align with a consistent vision across products and touchpoints. For companies committed to User-Centered Design (UCD), well-defined design principles ensure that every interaction, visual, and experience resonates with both the brand's identity and users' expectations.

This chapter explores the purpose and importance of design principles, provides examples from leading companies, and discusses how to create meaningful design principles that can shape user-centered products.

The Purpose of Design Principles

Design principles are a set of guiding statements that define a brand's design ethos, outlining what good design looks like for that company. They provide a framework for decision-making, helping designers resolve questions about aesthetics, functionality, and usability in a way that reflects the brand's values. Design principles are particularly important in complex or large organizations, where diverse teams work on different parts of a product or across multiple products. These principles ensure alignment, allowing each team to create a cohesive user experience that feels unified.

The main benefits of design principles in UCD include:

1. **Consistency Across Touchpoints**
   Design principles ensure that every product and feature aligns with a unified vision, creating a consistent experience for users. This cohesion reinforces brand identity, builds trust, and makes the product easier to learn and use.

2. **Clear Decision-Making**
   By outlining what matters most in design, principles help designers make consistent, user-centered decisions, even when faced with complex challenges. Design principles act as a touchstone, simplifying choices by providing clarity and focus.

3. **User-Centered Focus**
   Effective design principles keep the user at the center of the design process, guiding teams to make choices that address real user needs. This approach ensures that design decisions aren't just aesthetically pleasing but also functional and meaningful.

4. **Enhanced Collaboration**

   Design principles provide a common language for designers, developers, and stakeholders, facilitating collaboration and alignment. When everyone works with the same set of values, it's easier to create designs that resonate with both users and internal teams.

5. **Flexibility and Innovation**

   Rather than dictating specific styles or elements, design principles provide a high-level framework that allows for creative freedom. Designers can explore new ideas and adapt to evolving user needs while staying true to the brand's core values.

Examples of Notable Design Principles from Leading Companies

Many companies have created design principles that guide their approach to product development, user experience, and visual design. These principles offer valuable insights into the strategic priorities of each brand and provide a benchmark for creating impactful, user-centered designs.

1. Apple: Human, Intuitive, Clean

Apple's design principles reflect its focus on simplicity, clarity, and a human-centered approach. Known for its "less is more" philosophy, Apple's principles prioritize functionality and elegance, ensuring every design is accessible and approachable.

- **Human:** Apple emphasizes empathy and accessibility, creating products that feel intuitive and natural.
- **Intuitive:** Apple designs products that are easy to understand and navigate, even for first-time users.
- **Clean:** Apple values simplicity, using minimalistic design elements to reduce distractions and focus on functionality.

Reference: Apple Inc., *Human Interface Guidelines*. Retrieved from https://developer.apple.com/design/human-interface-guidelines.

2. Google: Focus on the User, Simplicity, Beauty, and Utility

Google's design principles prioritize user-centered design, simplicity, and utility, reflecting the company's mission to make information universally accessible. Google's Material Design principles highlight clarity and purpose, focusing on creating products that users can navigate easily.

- **Focus on the User:** Google places user needs at the forefront, aiming to solve real-world problems and anticipate user needs.
- **Simplicity and Beauty:** Design should be visually appealing yet functional, without unnecessary elements.
- **Utility:** Google's products are designed to be useful and helpful, prioritizing functionality over aesthetic alone.

Reference: Google. (2014). *Material Design*. Retrieved from https://material.io/design.

3. Microsoft: Inclusive, Adaptable, Secure, and Trusted

Microsoft's design principles reflect its focus on inclusivity, adaptability, and user security. The company's Fluent Design System prioritizes accessibility and flexibility, ensuring that Microsoft products are usable by a diverse range of people on multiple platforms.

- **Inclusive:** Design is accessible and usable for people of all abilities, reflecting Microsoft's commitment to inclusivity.
- **Adaptable:** Products are flexible, supporting seamless experiences across devices and input types.
- **Secure and Trusted:** Security and user privacy are prioritized, with design choices that help users feel safe.

Reference: Microsoft, *Fluent Design System*. Retrieved from https://www.microsoft.com/design/fluent.

4. Atlassian: Don't Make Me Think, Be Consistent, Think End-to-End

Atlassian's design principles are rooted in simplicity, consistency, and user-centric thinking. Known for collaboration tools like Jira and Confluence, Atlassian's principles prioritize ease of use and clarity, creating experiences that empower users to focus on their work.

- **Don't Make Me Think:** Designs should be simple, allowing users to navigate intuitively without unnecessary complexity.
- **Be Consistent:** Consistent design elements build familiarity and reduce cognitive load.

- **Think End-to-End:** Every touchpoint should contribute to a cohesive, seamless experience.

Reference: Atlassian, *Design Principles*. Retrieved from https://www.atlassian.design.

5. Airbnb: Unified, Universal, Iconic, and Conversational

Airbnb's design principles focus on creating a unique, approachable experience that aligns with the brand's mission to connect people and cultures. By emphasizing unity, approachability, and human-centered design, Airbnb's principles reflect its focus on creating a welcoming digital experience.

- **Unified:** Every aspect of the design aligns to provide a consistent, recognizable experience.
- **Universal:** Airbnb designs with inclusivity in mind, ensuring that people from different backgrounds feel comfortable using the platform.
- **Iconic and Conversational:** The design speaks in a clear, human tone, reflecting the approachable and friendly personality of the brand.

Reference: Airbnb, *Design Language System*. Retrieved from https://airbnb.design.

Creating Effective Design Principles for Your Brand

Creating meaningful design principles requires a deep understanding of both user needs and brand values. Effective design principles are clear, actionable, and rooted in empathy, offering guidance without restricting creativity. Here are some key steps for developing design principles that align with your brand and product goals.

1. Understand the Brand's Core Values

Design principles should be an extension of the brand's identity, reflecting what the company stands for and its unique value proposition. Collaborate with stakeholders to identify the brand's core values, discussing how these values might translate into design decisions.

- **Tip:** Start with a brand workshop or brainstorming session to capture values and vision. Ask questions like, "What do we want users to feel?" or "What makes our brand unique?"

2. Identify User Needs and Pain Points

User-centered design principles are grounded in a deep understanding of user needs. Use insights from research and discovery phases, including user personas, pain points, and behavioral data, to inform principles that prioritize usability and empathy.

- **Tip:** Align design principles with specific user goals or challenges. For example, if users find the product difficult to navigate, consider principles that emphasize simplicity and clarity.

3. Define Key Themes and Priorities

Design principles should be broad enough to guide decision-making across different scenarios but specific enough to provide clear direction. Aim for three to five principles that reflect the brand's focus, prioritizing themes like accessibility, simplicity, or consistency.

- **Tip:** Test each principle by asking, "Does this principle align with our brand values and user needs?" Eliminate any principles that feel redundant or overly vague.

4. Make Principles Actionable and Memorable

Design principles are more effective when they are easy to remember and actionable. Aim for clear, concise language that encourages specific behaviors, such as "Simplify, don't complicate" or "Design for everyone." Memorable language helps keep principles top-of-mind for the team.

- **Tip:** Use active verbs and straightforward language. For example, instead of "Prioritize simplicity," try "Make it easy."

5. Create Examples and Guidelines

For each principle, include examples or guidelines that illustrate how to apply it in practice. For instance, if a principle emphasizes "Accessibility for All," provide specific guidelines on color contrast, font size, and keyboard navigation.

- **Tip:** Use real design examples, such as screens, layouts, or interaction patterns, to demonstrate each principle in action. This helps make abstract ideas more tangible and applicable.

Implementing Design Principles in Daily Work

Once established, design principles should be embedded into the design process and referenced frequently. Encourage teams to use the principles as a lens for evaluating decisions, testing prototypes, and collaborating with stakeholders.

1. **Integrate Principles into the Design Review Process:** During design critiques, assess each decision against the design principles to ensure alignment. Use principles as a framework for providing feedback and resolving debates about design direction.

2. **Incorporate Principles in User Testing and Evaluation:** When conducting usability testing, use design principles as part of the evaluation criteria. Gather user feedback on whether the design meets the intentions behind each principle, and make adjustments as needed.

3. **Communicate Principles Across Teams:** Design principles are most effective when embraced by the entire organization, not just the design team. Share the principles with development, marketing, and product teams, and encourage them to apply the principles in their work.

Why Design Principles Matter in UCD

Design principles are foundational to User-Centered Design because they guide every decision, from layout to functionality, with the user's needs in mind. When principles are clear and actionable, they empower teams to make decisions that reflect a shared vision, improving both product consistency and user experience. For users, well-implemented design principles create a seamless, intuitive journey that feels cohesive, accessible, and aligned with the brand's values.

For designers, design principles provide a sense of purpose and clarity, enabling them to work creatively within a structured framework. In a rapidly changing digital landscape, design principles are a constant—ensuring that no matter how products evolve, they remain grounded in a user-centered approach.

By anchoring their work in thoughtful, user-centered design principles, teams can create products that are not only functional and aesthetically pleasing but also meaningful and impactful in the lives of users.

10 Usability Heuristics

Usability heuristics are general rules of thumb that help designers create intuitive, user-friendly interfaces. Developed to guide design decisions, these heuristics highlight common pitfalls and best practices, providing a framework for evaluating whether a product is easy to navigate, learn, and use. For companies focused on User-Centered Design (UCD), usability heuristics offer a quick, efficient way to identify potential usability issues early in the design process and ensure that designs meet user expectations.

In this chapter, we'll explore the importance of usability heuristics in UCD, look at notable heuristics from leading companies, and discuss how designers can apply these principles to enhance usability and user satisfaction.

The Purpose of Usability Heuristics

Usability heuristics serve as guidelines for creating intuitive, accessible, and user-centered designs. While they don't provide specific design solutions, heuristics help designers evaluate whether an interface is likely to meet users' needs and prevent common usability issues. Usability heuristics are particularly useful during the early stages of design and throughout the iterative process, as they provide a quick checklist for assessing potential pain points.

The primary benefits of using usability heuristics in UCD include:

1. **Early Problem Detection**
   Heuristics allow designers to identify and address usability issues before they reach users. By using heuristics as a checklist, designers can anticipate and resolve problems early, reducing the need for extensive rework after user testing.

2. **Guidance for Decision-Making**
   Heuristics offer a reference for making user-centered design decisions, providing clear principles that ensure a product aligns with usability standards. For example, if a design element doesn't match the heuristic of "visibility of system status," designers might reconsider the way it's displayed.

3. **Improved User Experience**
   Heuristics focus on core aspects of usability, such as error prevention, feedback, and consistency. By following these principles, designers create products that are easier to learn, navigate, and use, improving overall user satisfaction.

4. **Efficiency in Design and Development**
   Heuristics help streamline the design process by providing clear usability standards. Designers and developers can use heuristics as a quick reference, saving time by reducing the need for trial and error when making design choices.

5. **Foundation for Usability Testing**
   Usability heuristics offer a framework for heuristic evaluation, a form of expert usability testing where evaluators review the design against each heuristic. This approach provides a structured, efficient way to assess the usability of a design without requiring extensive user testing.

Key Usability Heuristics

Jakob Nielsen, a usability consultant and co-founder of the Nielsen Norman Group, developed a set of 10 widely accepted usability heuristics in the 1990s. These heuristics remain a foundation for user-centered design today, and many companies have since adapted them to create their own usability principles. Let's review Nielsen's 10 usability heuristics along with notable examples from prominent companies.

1. Visibility of System Status

The system should always keep users informed about what is happening through timely feedback. Users feel more comfortable and in control when they're aware of the system's status, especially during loading or processing times.

- **Example:** Google's search interface shows a loading spinner and provides visual feedback if a search takes longer than expected, indicating that the system is actively working on the request.

Reference: Nielsen, J. (1994). *10 Usability Heuristics for User Interface Design*. Retrieved from https://www.nngroup.com/articles/ten-usability-heuristics

2. Match Between System and the Real World

The design should use language, symbols, and conventions that align with users' real-world experiences. Interfaces that reflect users' expectations are easier to navigate and understand.

- **Example:** Airbnb uses familiar terminology, icons, and imagery in its booking process (e.g., "check-in" and "check-out" terms in a calendar format), aligning with the mental model of booking a hotel or accommodation.

3. User Control and Freedom

Users should be able to undo or exit actions to prevent mistakes. Offering ways to backtrack or cancel actions allows users to feel more in control, reducing anxiety about making errors.

- **Example:** Adobe's creative software provides an extensive "Undo" feature, along with keyboard shortcuts, to help users easily reverse actions and experiment without fear of losing work.

4. Consistency and Standards

Users shouldn't have to wonder if different words, icons, or actions mean the same thing. Consistent design and adherence to conventions make interfaces easier to learn and use.

- **Example:** Microsoft's Fluent Design System ensures consistency across all Microsoft products, creating a unified experience where users recognize icons, navigation patterns, and colors across Office, Windows, and other applications.

Reference: Microsoft, *Fluent Design System*. Retrieved from https://www.microsoft.com/design/fluent

5. Error Prevention

Designs should minimize the chance of user errors by making it difficult to make mistakes and offering clear prompts when errors might occur. This heuristic emphasizes preventing errors before they happen.

- **Example:** Shopify's interface includes built-in form validation, warning users when fields are incomplete or contain incorrect data before submission, preventing potential errors and frustration.

Reference: Shopify, *Polaris Design System*. Retrieved from https://polaris.shopify.com

6. Recognition Rather than Recall

Users should not have to remember information from one part of the interface to another. Designs that emphasize recognition help users by displaying visible options and familiar cues, minimizing cognitive load.

- **Example:** Amazon's "Recently Viewed" section allows users to quickly recognize and return to products they've previously browsed without relying on memory, enhancing convenience and ease of navigation.

7. Flexibility and Efficiency of Use

The design should accommodate both novice and experienced users. Advanced users may benefit from shortcuts or customization options that speed up frequent tasks.

- **Example:** Figma offers customizable keyboard shortcuts and plugin support, allowing advanced users to streamline their workflows and achieve greater efficiency.

Reference: Figma, *Design Principles and Shortcuts*. Retrieved from https://help.figma.com

8. Aesthetic and Minimalist Design

Designs should avoid clutter and only present essential information to prevent distraction. Minimalist design focuses on clarity and functionality, ensuring users can focus on core tasks without unnecessary visual elements.

- **Example:** Apple's product interfaces are known for their minimalist approach, presenting only essential information and interactions on each screen, allowing users to stay focused on their tasks.

Reference: Apple Inc., *Human Interface Guidelines*. Retrieved from https://developer.apple.com/design/human-interface-guidelines

9. Help Users Recognize, Diagnose, and Recover from Errors

Error messages should be clear, concise, and provide actionable solutions. Users should be able to understand what went wrong and how to fix it.

- **Example:** Slack provides friendly, straightforward error messages with suggested solutions, such as checking internet connectivity or re-entering login information, to help users resolve issues independently.

Reference: Slack, *Help Center*. Retrieved from https://slack.com/help

10. Help and Documentation

Although it's best to design systems that are intuitive, there may still be times when users need assistance. Providing accessible help and documentation enables users to find answers and complete tasks efficiently.

- **Example:** Atlassian's Confluence provides context-sensitive help links and a robust search function within its help center, enabling users to find relevant documentation for specific tasks.

Reference: Atlassian, *Confluence Help Center*. Retrieved from https://confluence.atlassian.com

Applying Usability Heuristics in Design

Usability heuristics can be applied throughout the design and development process, providing a benchmark for creating intuitive, user-friendly interfaces. Here are a few ways to incorporate usability heuristics into design work:

1. Heuristic Evaluation

A heuristic evaluation involves having usability experts or designers evaluate a product against a set of usability heuristics. This technique identifies usability issues quickly and cost-effectively, allowing for iterative improvements before user testing.

- **Process:** Experts systematically review each screen and interaction against heuristics, documenting any violations and prioritizing issues based on severity.
- **Tip:** Conduct heuristic evaluations periodically throughout the design process to catch usability issues early and make adjustments before they reach users.

2. Incorporate Heuristics into Design Reviews

Design teams can use heuristics as a framework for evaluating each other's work during design critiques. By referencing specific heuristics, team members can provide actionable feedback and maintain a consistent focus on usability.

- **Process:** During design reviews, ask questions like, "Does this screen follow the principle of 'consistency and standards'?" or "Is there a way to help users 'recognize rather than recall' information?"
- **Tip:** Encourage team members to discuss how each heuristic aligns with specific user needs or use cases to reinforce a user-centered perspective.

3. Use Heuristics to Inform Usability Testing

Heuristics can also be a helpful reference when designing usability tests. By creating test tasks that align with each heuristic, designers can systematically evaluate whether the interface meets key usability standards.

- **Process:** Develop tasks that specifically address each heuristic, such as testing error recovery (for "error prevention") or navigation ease (for "recognition rather than recall").
- **Tip:** Use heuristic-based test findings to guide iterative improvements and ensure that each design choice aligns with user needs.

4. Integrate Heuristics in Documentation and Design Guidelines

By embedding heuristics into design documentation and guidelines, companies can ensure that all team members have a shared understanding of usability best practices. This approach aligns designers, developers, and stakeholders on core principles that prioritize usability.

- **Process:** Create a section in the design system that covers usability heuristics, explaining each one with examples relevant to the product.
- **Tip:** Encourage all team members, from product managers to developers, to review and reference these heuristics in their work.

Why Usability Heuristics Matter in UCD

Usability heuristics play an essential role in User-Centered Design, offering a consistent, accessible set of standards for creating products that are intuitive and user-friendly. By focusing on common usability principles, designers can quickly and effectively assess the quality of an interface, improving both the design process and the final product. Heuristics bridge the gap between design intuition and user research, providing a structured approach to creating experiences that are not only functional but enjoyable and easy to use.

For designers, usability heuristics are valuable tools for evaluating, iterating, and improving designs. When used in tandem with user research, they help teams build products that meet user expectations, reduce friction, and enhance overall satisfaction.

By integrating usability heuristics into the design process, teams ensure that each interface is accessible, intuitive, and user-centered—creating products that meet user needs and provide a seamless experience.

11 Designing for Accessibility

Designing for accessibility ensures that digital products are usable by everyone, including people with disabilities. In User-Centered Design (UCD), accessibility is a critical consideration because it prioritizes inclusivity, ensuring that all users, regardless of ability, can access and interact with the product. Accessibility is not only a moral and legal obligation but also a valuable design practice that enhances usability and broadens the audience for a product.

This chapter explores the importance of designing for accessibility, discusses common accessibility standards, and provides an overview of tools and technologies that help designers and developers create accessible experiences.

The Importance of Designing for Accessibility

Accessible design goes beyond compliance; it embodies the principles of empathy and inclusivity. By considering diverse user needs, designers create products that are functional, intuitive, and accessible for everyone. Accessibility also benefits users without disabilities, improving usability by enhancing elements like clarity, contrast, and navigation.

The key benefits of designing for accessibility in UCD include:

1. **Inclusivity and Equality**
   Accessible design empowers people with disabilities to access information and services independently. Accessibility promotes equality by providing equal access to digital experiences, ensuring that people with disabilities are not excluded.

2. **Legal Compliance**
   Many countries have regulations that require digital products to meet specific accessibility standards. In the United States, the Americans with Disabilities Act (ADA) and Section 508 mandate accessibility for public websites, while the European Union has the Web Accessibility Directive. Designing for accessibility helps companies comply with these regulations and avoid legal consequences.

3. **Enhanced Usability**
   Accessibility often leads to better overall usability by focusing on clarity, navigation, and readability. For example, ensuring adequate color contrast benefits users with low vision while also making text easier to read in various lighting conditions.

4. **Broader Audience Reach**

   When products are accessible, they reach a larger audience, including users with disabilities. According to the World Health Organization, over one billion people live with some form of disability. Designing for accessibility enables companies to connect with this significant user group.

5. **Improved SEO and Performance**

   Many accessibility practices, such as using semantic HTML and descriptive alt text, improve search engine optimization (SEO) and website performance. Accessible design elements help search engines better understand and index content, boosting visibility and discoverability.

Key Accessibility Standards and Guidelines

To create accessible designs, it's essential to follow established standards and guidelines that outline best practices for usability and accessibility. The Web Content Accessibility Guidelines (WCAG) are the primary reference for designing accessible websites and applications.

Web Content Accessibility Guidelines (WCAG)

The WCAG, developed by the World Wide Web Consortium (W3C), provides a set of guidelines for making web content more accessible to people with disabilities. WCAG is organized around four key principles, often summarized with the acronym **POUR**:

1. **Perceivable:** Information and user interface components must be presented in ways that users can perceive, such as providing

text alternatives for non-text content and ensuring that content is adaptable.

2. **Operable:** The user interface and navigation should be operable for all users, including those who rely on keyboard navigation. This includes providing keyboard access, ensuring enough time to complete tasks, and designing content that doesn't cause seizures.

3. **Understandable:** Information and the operation of the user interface must be understandable, including readable text, predictable navigation, and help for users to avoid or correct mistakes.

4. **Robust:** Content must be robust enough to be reliably interpreted by assistive technologies, such as screen readers, ensuring that the design works across various platforms and technologies.

Reference: W3C, *Web Content Accessibility Guidelines (WCAG)*. Retrieved from https://www.w3.org/WAI/standards-guidelines/wcag/

Common Accessibility Tools and Technologies

Numerous tools and technologies support designers and developers in creating accessible products. These tools help identify and address accessibility issues, test designs with assistive technologies, and ensure compliance with accessibility standards.

1. Color Contrast Checkers

Color contrast is a fundamental aspect of accessible design, ensuring that text and interactive elements are easy to read for users with low vision or color blindness. Contrast checkers evaluate color combinations to ensure they meet WCAG standards.

- **Examples:**
  - **WebAIM Contrast Checker:** A simple tool to check color contrast ratios according to WCAG standards.
    - *Link*: https://webaim.org/resources/contrastchecker
  - **Color Contrast Analyzer (CCA):** A downloadable tool by the Paciello Group that tests color contrast in desktop applications.
    - *Link*: https://www.tpgi.com/color-contrast-checker/

2. Screen Readers

Screen readers are assistive technologies that convert text on a screen into spoken words, enabling visually impaired users to navigate and understand content. Testing with screen readers helps designers ensure their designs are compatible with these tools.

- **Examples:**
  - **JAWS (Job Access With Speech):** One of the most widely used screen readers for Windows, supporting web and software applications.

- *Link*:
  https://www.freedomscientific.com/products/software/jaws/
  - **NVDA (NonVisual Desktop Access):** A free, open-source screen reader for Windows.
    - *Link*: https://www.nvaccess.org
  - **VoiceOver:** Apple's built-in screen reader for macOS and iOS, allowing designers to test accessibility on Apple devices.
    - *Link*:
      https://www.apple.com/accessibility/vision/

3. Keyboard Navigation Testing

Keyboard accessibility is essential for users who cannot use a mouse. Testing for keyboard navigation ensures that users can access and interact with all elements using the keyboard alone, using tabbing and keyboard shortcuts.

- **Examples:**
  - **Keyboard Accessibility Toolkit:** A guide that helps designers and developers implement keyboard-friendly navigation.
    - *Link*:
      https://webaim.org/techniques/keyboard/
  - **WebAIM Keyboard Testing:** Guidelines for testing keyboard navigation in web content.
    - *Link*: https://webaim.org/articles/keyboard/

4. Accessibility Auditing Tools

Automated accessibility auditing tools scan websites and applications for compliance with WCAG standards, identifying common accessibility issues and providing recommendations for improvement.

- **Examples:**
  - **WAVE (Web Accessibility Evaluation Tool):** An online tool by WebAIM that evaluates websites for accessibility issues and provides visual feedback on detected problems.
    - *Link*: https://wave.webaim.org
  - **Axe by Deque:** A comprehensive accessibility testing tool that integrates with browsers and development environments, offering detailed reports and recommendations.
    - *Link*: https://www.deque.com/axe/
  - **Lighthouse:** Google's open-source tool for auditing performance, accessibility, and SEO, available as a Chrome extension.
    - *Link*: https://developers.google.com/web/tools/ligh thouse

5. ARIA (Accessible Rich Internet Applications) Attributes

ARIA is a set of attributes that developers can add to HTML elements to improve accessibility. ARIA labels, roles, and properties help assistive technologies understand the structure and purpose of web content.

- **Examples:**
  - **ARIA Authoring Practices Guide:** A comprehensive guide from the W3C on using ARIA to improve web accessibility.
    - *Link*: https://www.w3.org/WAI/ARIA/apg/
  - **aXe Accessibility Checker:** A tool that checks for ARIA usage and compatibility with assistive technologies.
    - *Link*: https://chrome.google.com/webstore/detail/axe/lhdoppojpmngadmnindnejefpokejbdd

6. Assistive Technology Emulators

Assistive technology emulators simulate different accessibility scenarios, such as color blindness or low vision, allowing designers to see how their designs look to users with various disabilities.

- **Examples:**
  - **Stark:** A plugin for Figma, Sketch, and Adobe XD that simulates color blindness and checks contrast to ensure accessible design choices.

- - *Link*: https://www.getstark.co
  - ○ **Color Oracle:** A free color blindness simulator for macOS, Windows, and Linux that helps designers understand how people with color vision deficiencies perceive their designs.
    - *Link*: https://colororacle.org

Best Practices for Designing Accessible User Experiences

Creating accessible designs involves more than just following guidelines; it requires empathy and a commitment to inclusivity. Here are some best practices to ensure your designs are accessible to a broad audience.

1. Use Semantic HTML and ARIA Labels

Semantic HTML tags (like <header>, <nav>, and <button>) provide meaning and structure to web content, helping screen readers interpret and navigate pages. When necessary, use ARIA attributes to add additional context for assistive technologies.

- **Tip:** Always label form fields, buttons, and images with descriptive text and ARIA attributes to ensure clarity for screen readers.

2. Design with Sufficient Color Contrast

Ensure that text and interactive elements have sufficient contrast with their background to meet WCAG standards. Color contrast is especially important for users with low vision or color blindness.

- **Tip:** Use tools like WebAIM's Contrast Checker to test color combinations and ensure they meet a minimum contrast ratio of 4.5:1 for text.

3. Provide Keyboard Navigation and Shortcuts

Ensure that all interactive elements are accessible via the keyboard alone, using a logical tab order and visual indicators for focused elements. Keyboard accessibility is crucial for users with motor disabilities who cannot use a mouse.

- **Tip:** Regularly test your design with keyboard-only navigation to ensure that all content and functionality is accessible without a mouse.

4. Use Clear, Concise Language and Provide Text Alternatives

Write in simple, clear language to make content understandable for users with cognitive disabilities. Additionally, provide text alternatives (alt text) for images, audio, and video to ensure information is accessible to screen reader users.

- **Tip:** Ensure that alt text is descriptive and specific to the image's purpose, providing context without unnecessary detail.

5. Design Responsively for Different Devices and Screen Sizes

Responsive design ensures that content adapts to various screen sizes and orientations, making it accessible to users on different devices. This flexibility also benefits users who zoom in on text or use mobile devices with accessibility features.

- **Tip:** Test your design on multiple devices and screen sizes to ensure it remains accessible and user-friendly.

6. Conduct Usability Testing with Users with Disabilities

Whenever possible, conduct usability testing with users who have disabilities. This hands-on testing provides valuable insights into accessibility challenges and helps teams identify areas for improvement.

- **Tip:** Include users with a range of disabilities in testing, such as visual, auditory, motor, and cognitive disabilities, to ensure comprehensive feedback on accessibility.

Why Accessibility Matters in UCD

Designing for accessibility is a core tenet of User-Centered Design, prioritizing the needs of all users and creating products that everyone can enjoy. By designing with accessibility in mind, teams demonstrate a commitment to inclusivity, helping to remove barriers and provide equal access to digital experiences. Accessible design is not just beneficial for users with disabilities—it improves usability for everyone, ensuring a seamless, engaging, and user-friendly experience.

For designers, mastering accessibility is an essential skill that not only meets ethical and legal requirements but also enhances the quality and reach of their work. Accessibility reflects a deeper empathy and respect for users, making it a vital element of creating products that serve everyone.

Designing for accessibility is integral to creating inclusive, user-centered products. By leveraging the tools, standards, and best practices covered in this chapter, designers can ensure that their work is accessible, meaningful, and impactful for every user.

Accessibility (A11y) Tools

- W3C, *Web Content Accessibility Guidelines (WCAG)*. Retrieved from https://www.w3.org/WAI/standards-guidelines/wcag/
- WebAIM, *Color Contrast Checker*. Retrieved from https://webaim.org/resources/contrastchecker
- NV Access, *NVDA Screen Reader*. Retrieved from https://www.nvaccess.org
- Deque, *Axe Accessibility Checker*. Retrieved from https://www.deque.com/axe/
- Stark, *Color Blindness Simulator and Contrast Checker*. Retrieved from https://www.getstark.co

12 UI/UX Team Structures in Organizations

The structure of UI/UX teams varies widely across organizations, depending on factors such as company size, product scope, and design maturity. In a small startup, a UI/UX designer may be expected to wear many hats, handling everything from user research to visual design, often working independently or with minimal guidance. In contrast, a larger organization or enterprise might have specialized roles within a multidisciplinary team, where each member focuses on a specific area, such as interaction design, visual design, or content strategy. The way a company organizes its UI/UX team can significantly impact both the team's productivity and the quality of the final user experience.

This chapter explores how the nature of a UI/UX designer's work changes depending on the team structure, and discusses common organizational models, including centralized and embedded structures, which influence how UI/UX teams operate within enterprises.

UI/UX Team Structures in Small Startups

In a small startup, resources and staffing are often limited, requiring designers to work flexibly and take on multiple roles. A UI/UX designer in a startup may be responsible for end-to-end design tasks, from conducting user research and defining personas to creating high-fidelity mockups and prototyping. This broad responsibility fosters a "generalist" role where designers are expected to wear many hats and adapt to evolving priorities.

Characteristics of UI/UX Work in Startups

1. **Wide Range of Responsibilities**
   A UI/UX designer at a startup typically manages the entire design process, handling user research, interaction design, visual design, and usability testing. In some cases, they may also be involved in front-end development or marketing design tasks, depending on the company's needs.

2. **Fast-Paced Environment and Flexibility**
   Startups operate in a fast-paced, iterative environment, where designers are often required to quickly produce prototypes, make adjustments based on rapid feedback, and pivot to new directions if needed. This requires a high level of adaptability and a willingness to experiment with different design solutions.

3. **Close Collaboration with Founders and Developers**
   In startups, the UI/UX designer frequently works closely with

founders and developers, often collaborating on strategic decisions and feature prioritization. This proximity allows designers to gain insights into the business model and user needs but may also mean balancing design goals with immediate business objectives.

4. **Limited Access to Specialized Tools and Resources**
Startups may lack the budget for premium tools or dedicated research resources, so designers often rely on affordable or open-source tools and quick, low-cost user testing methods. They may need to be resourceful, using methods such as guerrilla testing or simple surveys to gather user feedback.

Advantages and Challenges in Startup Environments

Advantages:

- **Broader Skill Development:** Designers gain experience in multiple aspects of design and product development.
- **High Impact:** Designers have more direct influence on the product and company vision.
- **Flexibility:** Startups encourage a trial-and-error approach, allowing designers to experiment with solutions.

Challenges:

- **Risk of Burnout:** Managing multiple responsibilities can be exhausting, especially in a fast-paced environment.
- **Limited Mentorship:** With a smaller team, designers may lack access to specialized mentorship and feedback.

- **Resource Constraints:** Limited budgets can restrict access to tools and user research, affecting design quality.

UI/UX Team Structures in Larger Organizations

In larger organizations, UI/UX teams are often multidisciplinary, with specialized roles focusing on different aspects of the design process. A dedicated UI/UX designer may be one part of a broader team that includes other specialists, such as Interaction Designers, Visual Designers, Content Strategists, and Accessibility Designers. This allows each team member to focus on specific skill sets and responsibilities, contributing their expertise to create a polished, user-centered product.

Specialized Roles within a Multidisciplinary UI/UX Team

1. **Interaction Designer**
   Interaction Designers focus on the structure and behavior of interactive elements. They design user flows, wireframes, and interactive prototypes, ensuring that users can navigate the product efficiently and intuitively.

2. **Visual Designer**
   Visual Designers are responsible for the product's aesthetics, including color schemes, typography, and brand alignment. They work to create a visually appealing interface that aligns with the company's visual identity and design language.

3. **Content Strategist**
   Content Strategists craft the language and tone used throughout the product, making sure it aligns with the brand

voice and provides clear, accessible information. They may also work on microcopy, instructional content, and error messages.

4. **User Researcher**

   User Researchers conduct in-depth research to understand user needs, behaviors, and pain points. They design and execute studies, including user interviews, surveys, and usability testing, to provide data-driven insights that guide design decisions.

5. **Accessibility Designer**

   Accessibility Designers focus on ensuring that the product meets accessibility standards, such as WCAG, to make the interface usable by people with disabilities. They assess contrast, screen reader compatibility, keyboard navigation, and more to create an inclusive experience.

6. **UX Writer**

   UX Writers work closely with Content Strategists to craft concise, clear, and user-friendly copy that guides users through the interface, helping to reduce confusion and enhance user satisfaction.

Advantages and Challenges in Larger Teams

Advantages:

- **Specialization:** Each team member focuses on their area of expertise, leading to higher-quality design outcomes.
- **Mentorship and Collaboration:** Designers benefit from working alongside experts in their field, fostering skill development and cross-functional learning.

- **Access to Advanced Resources:** Larger budgets allow for premium tools, extensive user research, and thorough accessibility testing.

Challenges:

- **Coordination and Alignment:** Collaboration across specialized roles requires clear communication and alignment, which can be challenging in larger teams.
- **Risk of Silos:** Specialized roles can sometimes lead to siloed thinking, where designers become focused on their tasks without considering the broader user experience.
- **Bureaucratic Decision-Making:** Larger organizations may have more complex approval processes, potentially slowing down the design and iteration process.

Organizational Models for UI/UX Teams in Enterprises

In enterprise environments, UI/UX teams can be structured in various ways to balance autonomy and alignment. Two of the most common organizational models are **centralized** and **embedded** team structures, each with its benefits and challenges.

Centralized UI/UX Team Structure

In a centralized structure, all UI/UX professionals are part of a single, cohesive team that serves different departments or product teams. The centralized team works together, sharing knowledge, resources, and best practices, while collaborating with various departments on individual projects.

Characteristics:

- **Unified Design Vision:** A centralized team ensures a consistent design vision across the organization, as all designers work under the same leadership and share a common set of guidelines and principles.
- **Knowledge Sharing:** Centralized teams encourage collaboration, knowledge-sharing, and skill development, allowing designers to learn from one another and maintain a high level of design consistency.
- **Centralized Resources:** Tools, user research, and accessibility testing resources are pooled together, making them easily accessible to all team members.

Advantages:

- **Consistency:** Centralization promotes consistency in brand, design language, and user experience across all products.
- **Efficiency in Resource Use:** Resources and tools are shared, reducing duplication and optimizing budget use.
- **Career Growth and Mentorship:** Designers have access to broader mentorship opportunities and clearer career paths within the design team.

Challenges:

- **Less Product-Specific Focus:** Centralized teams may struggle to align deeply with specific product teams, which can impact understanding of unique user needs.
- **Slower Decision-Making:** Decision-making can be slower due to the need for approvals and coordination with multiple departments.

Example: IBM employs a centralized design team structure, where the IBM Design Program oversees consistency in user experience across various products, enforcing guidelines from its Carbon Design System [IBM Design, 2023].

Reference: IBM Design. *Carbon Design System*. Retrieved from https://www.carbondesignsystem.com

Embedded UI/UX Team Structure

In an embedded structure, UI/UX designers are distributed across different product teams, working closely with developers, product managers, and stakeholders on specific projects. Each product team has its own dedicated UI/UX resources, allowing for a deeper understanding of product-specific needs.

Characteristics:

- **Dedicated Product Knowledge:** Designers embedded in product teams develop a strong understanding of specific product requirements and user needs, enabling them to create highly relevant solutions.

- **Increased Autonomy:** Embedded teams can make decisions more quickly, as they work directly with product managers and developers to meet team objectives.
- **Cross-Functional Collaboration:** Designers work alongside other disciplines, fostering close collaboration and alignment within the product team.

Advantages:

- **Product Focused:** Embedded teams align closely with product goals, leading to designs that are tailored to specific user needs and contexts.
- **Faster Iteration:** Designers can respond to feedback and make changes more quickly, as they have direct access to product stakeholders.
- **Stronger Team Identity:** Designers develop strong bonds with their product teams, fostering a shared commitment to product success.

Challenges:

- **Inconsistent Design Language:** Without centralized oversight, design consistency across products may suffer, as each team may interpret design guidelines differently.
- **Duplication of Efforts:** Each team may invest in separate resources or tools, which can lead to redundant costs.

- **Limited Knowledge Sharing:** Designers may have fewer opportunities to collaborate or learn from other UI/UX team members, potentially leading to siloed practices.

Example: Atlassian uses an embedded design structure, where designers are part of specific product teams like Jira or Confluence, collaborating closely with developers and product managers. Atlassian's design system, however, helps maintain consistency across these products [Atlassian Design, 2023].

Reference: Atlassian Design. *Atlassian Design System*. Retrieved from https://atlassian.design

Hybrid UI/UX Team Structure

A hybrid structure combines elements of both centralized and embedded models, aiming to balance consistency and autonomy. In this structure, designers are embedded within product teams but have regular touchpoints with a central design leadership team that provides shared resources, training, and guidelines.

Characteristics:

- **Consistent Design Standards:** Centralized leadership establishes design standards and provides a design system, while embedded teams tailor their approach to specific product needs.
- **Cross-Team Collaboration:** Designers have regular meetings or workshops to share knowledge and align on best practices across teams.

- **Resource Sharing:** Specialized resources, such as user researchers or accessibility experts, may be centralized and allocated to teams as needed.

Advantages:

- **Best of Both Worlds:** Hybrid structures provide the product-focused benefits of embedded teams with the consistency and support of centralized oversight.
- **Efficient Resource Use:** Shared resources, such as user research and accessibility expertise, are used efficiently, reducing duplication.
- **Enhanced Knowledge Sharing:** Designers can work closely with product teams while still benefiting from a larger design community.

Challenges:

- **Complex Coordination:** Hybrid structures require clear communication and alignment between centralized and embedded teams, which can be complex to manage.
- **Potential Role Overlap:** Hybrid structures may lead to role overlap, where centralized and embedded responsibilities aren't always clearly defined.

Why UI/UX Team Structures Matter in UCD

The structure of a UI/UX team directly impacts how effectively designers can create user-centered products. Startups benefit from generalist roles where designers take ownership of the entire process, while larger organizations leverage specialized roles that allow each designer to focus deeply on their area of expertise. Organizational models, such as centralized, embedded, or hybrid structures, determine the degree of alignment, collaboration, and flexibility that UI/UX teams experience.

For designers, understanding different team structures and organizational models can help clarify expectations, foster career growth, and enable them to make a meaningful impact within their roles. For organizations, structuring UI/UX teams thoughtfully ensures that products not only meet business goals but also deliver consistent, high-quality user experiences.

By aligning team structure with company needs and design goals, organizations can empower their UI/UX teams to create products that truly resonate with users, delivering experiences that are functional, cohesive, and user-centered.

13 UI/UX Titles, Career Paths, and Levels

The UI/UX field offers a diverse career path with opportunities for specialization, leadership, and advancement. As designers gain experience, they can follow different tracks within their careers, with roles ranging from hands-on, technical positions to leadership roles focused on team and project management. These tracks, often referred to as the "technical track" and the "people management track," allow designers to choose between deepening their technical expertise and taking on broader team responsibilities.

In this chapter, we'll explore the typical career progression for UI/UX professionals, the differences between the technical and management tracks, and an overview of title levels. We'll also examine approximate salary ranges for these levels in different locales as of 2024, highlighting how compensation can vary based on location, experience, and skill set.

Career Paths in UI/UX: Technical Track vs. People Management Track

UI/UX professionals generally have two main career paths to choose from as they advance: the **technical track** and the **people management track**. Both paths offer unique opportunities and challenges, and choosing between them often depends on a designer's interests, strengths, and career goals.

The Technical Track

The technical track is for designers who want to remain deeply involved in the craft of UI/UX design, honing their expertise and taking on increasingly complex projects. Professionals on this track focus on building technical skills, solving intricate design challenges, and becoming experts in specialized areas such as interaction design, accessibility, or design systems.

Key Characteristics:

- **Focus on Craft and Expertise:** Designers continue to build their technical skills, often specializing in specific design areas (e.g., visual design, user research, accessibility).
- **Ownership of Complex Projects:** Technical track designers take on high-impact projects, offering creative solutions and innovating within their domain.
- **Influence without Direct Management:** Senior designers on the technical track may mentor junior designers and influence design direction but don't typically manage teams.

Typical Titles:

- Junior or Associate Designer
- Designer
- Senior Designer
- Lead Designer
- Principal Designer
- Senior Principal Designer

The People Management Track

The people management track is for designers who want to take on leadership roles, guiding teams, managing projects, and aligning design goals with broader business objectives. Professionals on this track develop skills in team management, project coordination, and cross-functional collaboration, focusing on empowering team members and driving the strategic direction of the design organization.

Key Characteristics:

- **Focus on Team Development and Project Management:** Managers focus on supporting the growth and productivity of their team, handling project prioritization, and coordinating with other departments.
- **Strategic and Organizational Influence:** Design managers work closely with product and engineering leaders, contributing to strategic decision-making and resource allocation.

- **Mentorship and Talent Development:** People managers are responsible for career development, mentorship, and performance evaluation within their teams.

Typical Titles:

- Manager of Design
- Senior Manager of Design
- Design Director
- Senior Design Director
- VP of Design
- Chief Design Officer

Typical Levels and Titles in UI/UX Career Paths

Here is an overview of common titles, from entry-level to executive, that UI/UX designers may encounter along their career paths. While specific titles can vary between organizations, this list represents a common hierarchy in both the technical and management tracks.

Entry-Level Positions

1. **Intern**
   - **Role:** Interns are typically students or recent graduates gaining hands-on experience. They work under the guidance of senior designers, assisting on projects, and learning foundational skills.
   - **Responsibilities:** Supporting design tasks, conducting user research, creating basic wireframes, and contributing to visual design work.

2. **Junior or Associate Designer**
   o **Role:** Junior designers have entry-level responsibilities, focusing on specific tasks and gradually developing their design skills. They work under supervision, learning design tools and techniques.
   o **Responsibilities:** Assisting in creating wireframes, prototypes, visual assets, and supporting user research activities.

Mid-Level Positions

3. **Designer (UI/UX Designer)**
   o **Role:** Mid-level designers have foundational skills in UI and UX and can handle small projects independently. They collaborate closely with other designers, developers, and product managers.
   o **Responsibilities:** Developing user flows, designing screens, conducting usability tests, and refining designs based on feedback.
4. **Senior Designer (Senior UI/UX Designer)**
   o **Role:** Senior designers are proficient in all aspects of UI/UX design and can lead projects with minimal supervision. They bring experience and a broader understanding of user-centered design principles.
   o **Responsibilities:** Leading projects, mentoring junior designers, conducting in-depth user research, and refining design systems.

5. **Lead Designer**
   - **Role:** Lead designers have deep expertise in UI/UX design and typically oversee project teams, ensuring that design work meets high standards and aligns with product goals.
   - **Responsibilities:** Setting project direction, collaborating on strategic design decisions, and overseeing the quality of deliverables.

Advanced and Specialist Positions

6. **Principal Designer**
   - **Role:** Principal designers are senior-level experts who focus on complex, high-impact projects. They have significant influence on design strategy and may guide multiple product teams.
   - **Responsibilities:** Leading critical projects, contributing to design systems, advising on strategic design decisions, and mentoring senior designers.
7. **Senior Principal Designer**
   - **Role:** This level represents further specialization and seniority, where designers are thought leaders within the organization. They may focus on long-term design vision and innovation.
   - **Responsibilities:** Setting design direction for the organization, working on advanced design systems, and influencing company-wide design standards.

Management Positions

8. **Manager of Design**
   - **Role:** Design managers oversee a team of designers, providing mentorship, handling project assignments, and aligning team work with business objectives.
   - **Responsibilities:** Managing team performance, supporting career development, collaborating with cross-functional partners, and facilitating design reviews.

9. **Senior Manager of Design**
   - **Role:** Senior managers manage larger teams and have greater responsibility for aligning design initiatives with organizational goals. They work closely with directors and executives on strategic priorities.
   - **Responsibilities:** Overseeing multiple design teams, setting team goals, managing budget and resources, and driving cross-functional initiatives.

Executive and Leadership Positions

10. **Design Director**
    - **Role:** Design directors lead the design department, setting the vision, goals, and standards. They work closely with senior leadership to ensure design aligns with business strategy.
    - **Responsibilities:** Driving the design strategy, managing high-level projects, representing the design team to executive stakeholders, and fostering a collaborative culture.

11. VP of Design

- ○ **Role:** The VP of Design is responsible for the entire design organization, ensuring that design functions support the company's strategic goals. This role often combines design leadership with executive responsibilities.
- ○ **Responsibilities:** Overseeing design direction, setting organizational goals, managing multiple design teams, and reporting directly to the C-suite.

12. Chief Design Officer (CDO)

- ○ **Role:** The CDO is an executive role that establishes the design vision for the entire organization, often with responsibilities across design, brand, and customer experience.
- ○ **Responsibilities:** Driving long-term design vision, aligning design with company mission, setting organization-wide standards, and advocating for design at the highest levels.

Salary Ranges for UI/UX Roles in 2024

As of 2024, salaries for UI/UX roles vary widely based on experience, title, and location. Below is an approximate salary range for each level across major tech hubs and remote roles.

Role	USA (San Francisco / NYC)	Europe (Berlin / London)	Asia (Singapore / Hong Kong)	Remote
Intern	$50,000 - $65,000	€25,000 - €35,000	SGD 30,000 - SGD 45,000	$40,000 - $50,000
Junior / Associate Designer	$70,000 - $90,000	€35,000 - €50,000	SGD 45,000 - SGD 65,000	$60,000 - $80,000
Designer	$90,000 - $110,000	€50,000 - €70,000	SGD 65,000 - SGD 90,000	$80,000 - $100,000
Senior Designer	$110,000 - $140,000	€70,000 - €90,000	SGD 90,000 - SGD 120,000	$100,000 - $130,000
Lead Designer	$140,000 - $170,000	€90,000 - €120,000	SGD 120,000 - SGD 150,000	$130,000 - $160,000
Principal Designer	$160,000 - $200,000	€100,000 - €140,000	SGD 140,000 - SGD 180,000	$140,000 - $180,000
Senior Principal Designer	$180,000 - $220,000	€120,000 - €160,000	SGD 160,000 - SGD 200,000	$160,000 - $200,000
Manager of Design	$140,000 - $180,000	€90,000 - €130,000	SGD 120,000 - SGD 160,000	$130,000 - $170,000
Senior Manager of Design	$160,000 - $200,000	€120,000 - €150,000	SGD 150,000 - SGD 180,000	$150,000 - $190,000
Design Director	$200,000 - $250,000	€140,000 - €180,000	SGD 180,000 - SGD 220,000	$180,000 - $220,000
VP of Design	$250,000 - $300,000	€180,000 - €220,000	SGD 220,000 - SGD 270,000	$200,000 - $260,000
Chief Design Officer	$300,000+	€220,000+	SGD 270,000+	$250,000+

Note: Salary ranges are approximate and can vary significantly based on company, industry, and individual qualifications. Remote salaries tend to align with cost of living adjustments, often falling between high-cost areas like San Francisco and lower-cost areas.

Why UI/UX Career Path and Levels Matter

Understanding the UI/UX career path, including technical and management tracks, helps designers navigate their career journeys, choose roles that align with their strengths, and identify growth opportunities. For organizations, establishing clear UI/UX roles and levels provides transparency, helping to attract, retain, and develop talent. With well-defined levels, UI/UX professionals can pursue their career goals, whether they aspire to master their craft as a Principal Designer or lead a design organization as a Chief Design Officer.

By offering both technical and people management tracks, companies empower designers to grow in ways that suit their individual skills and aspirations, creating a stronger, more versatile UI/UX community.

14 Applying for UI/UX Design Jobs

Applying for design jobs requires careful planning, from finding the right job opportunities to tailoring your resume and portfolio, preparing for interviews, and standing out to hiring managers. For UI/UX designers, a strong application reflects both technical skill and creativity, showcasing your design thinking, problem-solving abilities, and attention to detail. This chapter covers the key steps to landing a UI/UX role that fits your skills and career goals, from job search strategies to interview preparation.

Step 1: Finding the Right Job Opportunities

The first step in applying for a design job is to identify positions that align with your skills, career goals, and values. Different companies and roles require different skill sets, and understanding the requirements and culture of potential employers helps you focus on positions where you're most likely to thrive.

Job Search Strategies

1. **Job Boards and Platforms**
   Use specialized job boards that cater to design and tech roles to find UI/UX positions. Major platforms like LinkedIn and Indeed are useful, but niche job boards often provide more targeted opportunities.
   - **Resources:**
     - **Dribbble** (https://dribbble.com/jobs): A design-centric platform with job listings for UI/UX roles and creative positions.
     - **Behance Job Board** (https://www.behance.net/jobs): Adobe's Behance platform has a job board where companies seek designers across various disciplines.
     - **AngelList** (https://angel.co/jobs): A platform for jobs at startups, ideal for designers interested in working in fast-paced, innovative environments.
     - **Remote Design Jobs** (https://www.remotedesignjobs.co): A job board specifically for remote design roles, which has gained popularity in recent years.
2. **Company Websites**
   Many companies post job openings on their own careers pages.

If there are specific companies you're interested in, regularly check their websites or set up job alerts.

3. **Networking**

   Networking is essential for uncovering hidden job opportunities. Attend industry events, join online communities, and connect with professionals in the field. Platforms like LinkedIn, Slack communities (e.g., Designer Hangout, UX Design Community), and in-person events or conferences (e.g., AIGA, UXPA) are great for building connections.

4. **Design Communities and Social Media**

   Follow design communities, companies, and leaders on social media platforms like Twitter, LinkedIn, and Instagram. Companies often share job openings in these communities, and some roles are advertised exclusively on social channels.

Step 2: Preparing Your Resume

Your resume is the first impression you make on a hiring manager, so it's essential to highlight your relevant experience, skills, and achievements clearly and concisely. For UI/UX roles, your resume should reflect your design expertise, problem-solving abilities, and how you've contributed to successful design projects.

Key Elements of a Strong UI/UX Resume

1. **Clear Contact Information**

   Include your full name, phone number, email address,

LinkedIn profile, and portfolio link. Make sure these details are easy to find at the top of your resume.

2. **Professional Summary**
   Write a brief summary (2-3 sentences) that highlights your design background, core skills, and what you bring to the table. Focus on your unique value and experience level (e.g., "Senior UI/UX Designer with a strong focus on accessibility and user-centered design for digital products").

3. **Skills Section**
   List relevant skills, such as user research, wireframing, prototyping, interaction design, visual design, and specific design tools (e.g., Figma, Adobe XD, Sketch). Tailor this section to match the skills required in the job description.

4. **Professional Experience**
   Use bullet points to outline your past roles, starting with your most recent position. Focus on measurable achievements, such as "Increased conversion rates by 15% by redesigning the user onboarding flow." Highlight projects where you contributed to user-centered outcomes, collaborated with cross-functional teams, or led design efforts.

5. **Education and Certifications**
   Include any relevant degrees, certifications, or courses (e.g., HCI degree, UX design certification, Google UX Design Professional Certificate).

6. **Additional Information (Optional)**
   Include links to personal design projects, published articles, or design community involvement if relevant. Showcasing involvement in design events or personal projects demonstrates initiative and a commitment to growth.

Resources:

- **Resume Builders:** Canva (https://www.canva.com/resumes/), Adobe Express (https://www.adobe.com/express/create/resume) offer design-focused resume templates.
- **Examples and Inspiration:** Look at resume examples on Dribbble and Behance to see how other designers structure their resumes.

Step 3: Crafting an Impressive Design Portfolio

A portfolio is essential for UI/UX designers, as it showcases your work, design process, and creative thinking. Your portfolio should be user-friendly, visually appealing, and reflective of your strengths and areas of expertise. A well-curated portfolio tells a story about who you are as a designer and how you solve problems through design.

Essential Elements of a UI/UX Portfolio

1. **Case Studies**

   Each project in your portfolio should be presented as a case study that explains the design process from beginning to end. Case studies should include:

   - **Project Overview:** A brief summary of the project, your role, and the objective.
   - **Problem Statement:** Define the user problem you aimed to solve.

- Process: Describe your approach, including user research, wireframing, prototyping, and testing. Use visuals to showcase each stage.
- Solution: Present the final design, explaining how it solves the problem. Include high-fidelity mockups and prototypes.
- Outcome: If applicable, mention metrics or qualitative feedback that shows the project's success (e.g., improved user engagement, reduced onboarding time).

2. **Personal Projects**

   Personal projects, redesigns, or conceptual work are a great way to show creativity and initiative, especially if you're newer to the field. Include these as part of your portfolio to showcase your design skills and process.

3. **User-Friendly Design and Navigation**

   Your portfolio should reflect your UX skills, with intuitive navigation, clear labeling, and mobile responsiveness. Make it easy for hiring managers to browse your projects without friction.

4. **About Me Section**

   Include a brief "About Me" section that introduces you as a designer, highlights your skills, and describes what you're passionate about. This personal touch makes your portfolio memorable.

5. **Contact Information and Links**

   Include a clear way to contact you, such as an email link, and social media or LinkedIn links. Your contact information should be accessible from any page.

Portfolio Platforms:

- **Webflow** (https://webflow.com): Great for building custom, responsive portfolio sites without coding.
- **Squarespace** (https://www.squarespace.com): An intuitive platform with beautiful templates for creating design portfolios.
- **Behance** (https://www.behance.net): Popular for hosting portfolios and connecting with other designers.
- **Dribbble** (https://dribbble.com): Ideal for sharing snippets of your work and getting visibility in the design community.

Step 4: Navigating the UI/UX Interview Process

The UI/UX interview process often consists of several stages, including initial screening, portfolio reviews, design challenges, and behavioral interviews. Understanding each stage will help you prepare and make a strong impression.

Typical Stages of the UI/UX Interview Process

1. **Initial Screening**
   The initial screening, often conducted by a recruiter, assesses whether you have the skills and experience required for the role. This stage focuses on your background and fit with the company.
   Preparation:
   - Be ready to discuss your resume and explain your interest in the company and role.
   - Research the company's mission, values, and recent projects to show alignment with their goals.

2. **Portfolio Review**

   In the portfolio review, you'll present your portfolio and walk through specific projects, explaining your design process and decisions. Hiring managers look for your problem-solving abilities, communication skills, and understanding of user-centered design.

   Preparation:
   - Practice presenting each case study concisely, highlighting the problem, process, and results.
   - Be ready to answer questions about your design decisions, challenges you faced, and how you collaborated with others.

3. **Design Challenge or Whiteboard Exercise**

   Design challenges are common in UI/UX interviews and may involve a take-home assignment or a live exercise. This stage tests your ability to approach design problems, ideate, and communicate your thinking process.

   Preparation:
   - Familiarize yourself with common design challenge formats (e.g., redesigning a feature, creating a new user flow).
   - Use structured frameworks like the Double Diamond (Discover, Define, Develop, Deliver) or design thinking to organize your approach.
   - During live exercises, verbalize your thought process and involve the interviewer in your reasoning.

4. **Behavioral Interview**

   Behavioral interviews assess soft skills such as communication, teamwork, adaptability, and problem-solving. These questions often start with "Tell me about a time when…" and focus on how you handled specific situations.

Preparation:
- Use the STAR method (Situation, Task, Action, Result) to structure your responses.
- Prepare examples that demonstrate key skills, such as collaborating with developers, handling feedback, or working under tight deadlines.

5. **Final Round Interviews**

In final interviews, you may meet with senior designers, product managers, or executives. These interviews evaluate cultural fit, your long-term potential, and your alignment with the company's goals.

Preparation:
- Prepare thoughtful questions about the company culture, design process, and team dynamics.
- Express your vision for your role and how you plan **to contribute to the company's mission.**

Resources for Interview Prep:

- **UX Design Interviews:** *Cracking the UX Interview* by Ellie Dawes (Book).
- **Mock Interviews:** Try *Pramp* (https://www.pramp.com) or *Interviewing.io* (https://interviewing.io) to practice interview skills.
- **STAR Method:** Learn more about the STAR method (https://www.themuse.com/advice/star-interview-method) for behavioral interviews.

Final Tips for a Successful UI/UX Job Application

1. **Tailor Your Application:** Customize your resume and portfolio to highlight the skills and experience most relevant to each position.

2. **Showcase Soft Skills:** Effective communication, adaptability, and collaboration are essential in UI/UX roles, so demonstrate these qualities in your portfolio and interviews.

3. **Prepare Thoughtful Questions:** Asking questions about the design team, workflows, and company culture shows genuine interest and helps you evaluate fit.

4. **Follow Up:** After each interview, send a thank-you note expressing appreciation for the opportunity to learn about the role and your excitement for the potential fit.

Summary

Applying for UI/UX roles requires more than technical skill. By identifying the right roles, crafting a compelling resume and portfolio, and preparing strategically for each stage of the interview process, you can set yourself apart as a candidate who's both talented and thoughtfully engaged. The right preparation not only enhances your chances of landing a job but also positions you for long-term success in the dynamic and rewarding field of UI/UX design.

15 New Opportunities for Designers in the Age of AI

As artificial intelligence (AI) becomes increasingly integrated into products and services, designers are presented with new opportunities to shape innovative, user-centered experiences that leverage AI's unique capabilities. AI can transform the way we approach problems, automate routine tasks, personalize interactions, and make data-driven decisions. Designers equipped with user-centered design skills are well-positioned to uncover valuable ways AI can solve real-world challenges for businesses and users alike. This chapter explores how UI/UX designers can adapt their skills for AI, discusses key tools and no-code/low-code platforms for designing AI-driven solutions, and highlights resources to help designers learn more about AI.

Why User-Centered Design is Essential for AI Solutions

AI is a powerful tool, but without a thoughtful, user-centered approach, it can lead to overly complex, impersonal, or even harmful user experiences. Designers with a strong foundation in user-centered design (UCD) are uniquely qualified to bring a human perspective to AI projects, ensuring that AI applications solve meaningful problems, are easy to use, and feel trustworthy.

Key ways in which UCD skills enhance AI-driven design include:

1. **Problem Definition and User Research**
   The first step in designing an effective AI solution is understanding the problem from the user's perspective. User Experience (UX) designers are skilled in conducting user research, uncovering pain points, and defining clear goals. This user-centered approach ensures that AI solutions are designed to address genuine user needs rather than just showcasing technological capabilities.

2. **Mapping User Journeys and Designing Interactions**
   Designing AI-driven experiences requires careful consideration of when and how AI should be involved in the user journey. UX designers excel at mapping out user flows and identifying the right touchpoints for AI interventions, whether that involves automating a repetitive task, providing personalized recommendations, or enabling voice-activated interactions.

3. **Ethics and Transparency in AI**
   With AI, especially in areas like generative AI and data-driven

personalization, ethical concerns about privacy, bias, and transparency arise. UX designers bring empathy and ethical consideration to AI projects, ensuring that solutions are transparent, fair, and respect user privacy.

4. **Designing for Explainability and Trust**
   As AI-driven interfaces become more sophisticated, users need to trust that the system is making appropriate decisions. Designers play a critical role in crafting interactions that explain AI-driven actions, helping users understand and feel in control of automated processes.

5. **Rapid Prototyping and Iteration**
   AI is an evolving field, and prototyping AI-powered solutions requires experimentation and iteration. Designers' experience in rapid prototyping and usability testing ensures that AI features are user-friendly and refined based on real feedback.

Building AI Skills: Learning Resources for Designers

Transitioning into AI-driven design doesn't require deep technical knowledge of algorithms or programming. Instead, designers can start by learning the basics of AI, focusing on applications, ethics, and no-code/low-code tools for prototyping AI-driven experiences. Here are some resources to get started:

1. Foundations of AI and Machine Learning
   - **Google's Machine Learning Crash Course:** A free course designed for beginners, covering the basics of machine learning concepts and applications.
     - *Link*: https://developers.google.com/machine-learning/crash-course
   - **Elements of AI:** A comprehensive online course that introduces AI concepts, ethics, and applications, created by the University of Helsinki.
     - *Link*: https://www.elementsofai.com

2. AI for Designers
   - **UX Design for AI:** An online course by Coursera, which focuses on applying UX principles to AI and data-driven products.
     - *Link*: https://www.coursera.org/learn/ai-for-everyone
   - **Interaction Design Foundation (IDF) - AI for Designers:** A course tailored specifically for designers looking to apply user-centered principles to AI products.
     - *Link*: https://www.interaction-design.org

3. AI Ethics and Design
   - **AI Ethics for Designers:** This article series by Nielsen Norman Group covers ethical considerations and best practices for designing AI applications.

- *Link*:
   https://www.nngroup.com/articles/ai-ethics-d
   esign/
4. **Generative AI Tools for Prototyping**
   - **OpenAI Documentation and Tutorials:** Get started with generative AI by experimenting with OpenAI's models like ChatGPT, DALL-E, and Codex.
     - *Link*: https://platform.openai.com/docs
   - **Anthropic's Claude:** An alternative generative AI tool to ChatGPT, Claude focuses on being helpful and safe, with a more conservative approach to large language models.
     - *Link*: https://www.anthropic.com

Experimenting with No-Code/Low-Code AI Tools

No-code and low-code platforms make it easy for designers to prototype and build AI-driven solutions without needing advanced programming skills. These tools enable designers to integrate AI features like chatbots, workflow automation, and data insights into prototypes, allowing rapid experimentation with AI capabilities.

1. Voiceflow for Conversational AI and Chatbots

Voiceflow is a no-code platform for creating conversational experiences, allowing designers to build and test voice assistants, chatbots, and AI-driven customer service tools. Designers can use Voiceflow to create complex conversational flows, integrate AI models, and prototype for platforms like Alexa and Google Assistant.

- **Key Features:** Drag-and-drop interface, API integrations, support for complex conversation flows.
- **Use Cases:** Creating customer service chatbots, designing interactive voice experiences, prototyping AI-driven customer support tools.
- *Link*: https://www.voiceflow.com

2. Zapier and Make for Workflow Automation

Zapier and Make (formerly Integromat) are popular automation platforms that allow designers to integrate AI capabilities into workflows and automate tasks across multiple applications. These tools help streamline repetitive tasks, enabling designers to prototype solutions that integrate data-driven insights or AI-powered automation.

- **Key Features:** Pre-built integrations with hundreds of apps, conditional logic, workflow customization.
- **Use Cases:** Automating user notifications, creating AI-powered data pipelines, generating automated reports.
- *Links*:
  - Zapier: https://zapier.com
  - Make (Integromat): https://www.make.com

3. Relevance AI for Data-Driven Insights

Relevance AI is a platform for analyzing unstructured data using AI. Designers can use Relevance AI to build prototypes that integrate data analysis and machine learning insights, uncovering patterns, clustering data, and visualizing insights without needing to write complex code.

- **Key Features:** No-code data visualization, clustering and tagging, unstructured data analysis.
- Use Cases: Prototyping user analytics dashboards, clustering customer feedback, analyzing social media trends.
- *Link*: https://www.relevance.ai

4. OpenAI and Google Gemini for Generative AI

OpenAI and Google Gemini offer consumer-focused generative AI tools, including text generation, image synthesis, and interactive chatbots. Designers can experiment with these tools to generate content, brainstorm design concepts, or create interactive AI prototypes that respond to user inputs.

- **Key Features:** Text generation, image synthesis, chatbot integration.
- **Use Cases:** Prototyping AI-driven customer service bots, creating content recommendation systems, generating custom images for prototypes.
- *Links*:
  - OpenAI (ChatGPT, DALL-E): https://platform.openai.com
  - Google Gemini: https://ai.google

Practical Examples of AI-Driven Solutions for Designers

Here are some practical ways UI/UX designers can start applying AI to solve business problems or enhance user experiences:

1. **Designing Personalized User Experiences**
   Designers can use AI to create personalized recommendations, automate content suggestions, and deliver customized experiences. For example, by analyzing user behavior data, designers can create a personalized interface that displays relevant content or recommendations based on user preferences.

2. **Building Conversational Interfaces and Chatbots**
   Conversational AI allows users to interact with products through natural language. Designers can use tools like Voiceflow to create chatbots that handle user inquiries, guide onboarding, or assist with navigation. This provides a hands-on way to explore the potential of conversational interfaces without needing to write complex scripts.

3. **Automating User Feedback Analysis**
   Relevance AI and similar tools can analyze large volumes of user feedback, clustering similar comments, tagging themes, and visualizing insights. This enables designers to quickly identify recurring issues, user preferences, or feature requests, helping to make data-driven design improvements.

4. **Enhancing Accessibility with AI**
   AI-powered tools can make interfaces more accessible. For

example, designers can use AI to generate automated captions, adapt layouts based on user preferences, or provide image descriptions for visually impaired users. Experimenting with accessible design tools helps designers create inclusive experiences.

5. **Prototyping Dynamic Content with Generative AI**
Generative AI can be used to prototype interfaces that respond to user input with dynamically generated content. For example, using OpenAI's ChatGPT or Google Gemini, designers can build a mockup of a customer support bot that answers frequently asked questions, helping them explore how AI-generated responses might enhance customer interactions.

Resources for Expanding Your AI Design Skills

1. **AI and Design Books**
   - Designing with AI by Smashing Magazine: This book explores how designers can approach AI from a user-centered perspective, covering the principles of designing intuitive AI solutions.
   - Data-Driven UX Design by Pamella Neely: A guide to using data in UX, this book is ideal for designers interested in data-driven insights to inform AI-powered solutions.
2. **AI and Design Communities**
   - AI for Designers on LinkedIn: A group where designers discuss AI trends, tools, and best practices.

- UX Collective's AI Section: UX Collective has a section dedicated to articles and resources on AI for designers.
  - *Link*: https://uxdesign.cc/tagged/ai
3. **Prototyping and Design Tools with AI Integrations**
   - Figma with AI Plugins: Figma offers plugins like Content Reel for generating text and Lottie for adding animations, making it easier to prototype AI-driven experiences.
     - *Link*: https://www.figma.com/community
   - Canva Magic Design: Canva's AI-powered tool lets designers experiment with AI-generated design elements and layouts.
     - *Link*: https://www.canva.com

The Future of AI and Design

AI's potential to transform the design industry is vast, and the role of designers will continue to evolve as AI technology advances. By staying informed, experimenting with no-code tools, and applying user-centered design principles to AI solutions, designers can contribute to meaningful, user-friendly innovations. For UI/UX professionals, embracing AI offers a pathway to expand skills, tackle complex problems, and shape the future of digital experiences in a way that serves both business objectives and user needs.

References

Apple Developer Documentation. (n.d.). *Human interface guidelines.* Retrieved from https://developer.apple.com/design/human-interface-guidelines/

Atlassian Design System. (n.d.). *Design principles.* Retrieved from https://atlassian.design/

Carbon Design System. (n.d.). *Carbon Design System.* Retrieved from https://carbondesignsystem.com/

Deque. (2024, June 3). *Axe: Accessibility testing tools and software.* Retrieved from https://www.deque.com/axe/

Fluent 2 Design System. (n.d.). *Fluent 2 design system.* Retrieved from https://fluent2.microsoft.design/

Material Design. (n.d.). *Material design.* Retrieved from https://m3.material.io/

Nielsen, J. (2024, February 20). *10 usability heuristics for user interface design.* Nielsen Norman Group. Retrieved from https://www.nngroup.com/articles/ten-usability-heuristics/

Nielsen Norman Group. (n.d.). *Usability engineering: Book by Jakob Nielsen.* Retrieved from https://www.nngroup.com/books/usability-engineering/

Norman, D. (2004). *Emotional design: Why we love (or hate) everyday things.* Basic Books.

NV Access. (n.d.). *NVDA screen reader.* Retrieved from https://www.nvaccess.org

Shopify. (n.d.). *Polaris design system.* Retrieved from https://polaris.shopify.com

Sprint: How to solve big problems and test new ideas in just five days. (2016). Bantam Press.

Stark. (n.d.). *Color blindness simulator and contrast checker.* Retrieved from https://www.getstark.co

W3C. (n.d.). *Web content accessibility guidelines (WCAG).* Retrieved from https://www.w3.org/WAI/standards-guidelines/wcag/

WebAIM. (n.d.). *Color contrast checker.* Retrieved from https://webaim.org/resources/contrastchecker